WONDER

The University of North Carolina Press ✳ CHAPEL HILL

WONDER

From Emotion to Spirituality ✳ ROBERT C. FULLER

Designed by Rebecca Gimenez

Set in Minion by Keystone Typesetting, Inc.

Manufactured in the United States of America

This book was published with the assistance
of the William R. Kenan Jr. Fund of the University
of North Carolina Press.

The paper in this book meets the guidelines
for permanence and durability of the Committee
on Production Guidelines for Book Longevity
of the Council on Library Resources.

Library of Congress Cataloging-in-Publication Data
Fuller, Robert C., 1952–
Wonder : from emotion to spirituality / Robert C. Fuller.
p. cm.
Includes bibliographical references and index.
ISBN-13: 978-0-8078-2995-0 (cloth : alk. paper)
ISBN-10: 0-8078-2995-1 (cloth : alk. paper)
1. Awe. 2. Wonder. 3. Emotions—Religious aspects.
4. Psychology, Religious. 5. Experience (Religion)
6. Evolution (Biology) I. Title.
BF575.A9F85   2006
204'.2—dc22   2005016885

10 09 08 07 06   5 4 3 2 1

CONTENTS

PREFACE

M Y INTEREST IN THE LINK BETWEEN WONDER AND spirituality has many sources. I have been studying the psychology of religion for more than thirty years and have spent a great deal of time trying to understand the inner causes of religious experience or belief. It was, however, two fairly recent conversations that prompted me to investigate the role of wonder in the origins of human spirituality. The first was an extended conversation I had with Karen Armstrong, the author of several best-selling books on religion. Karen was finishing a book on religious fundamentalism, a project that made her acutely aware of the cultural problems created by religions that believe they possess a monopoly on truth. Karen concluded that we are probably wrong to expect religion to possess truth in the first place. She reasoned that the real purpose of religion has nothing to do with factual truth. Karen ventured that the purpose of religion is instead about "holding us in a state of wonder." She didn't elaborate on what she meant by this, but its basic point seemed clear. Religious beliefs and rituals aren't about truth if by that we mean propositions that can be validated as factual in a way similar to propositions in mathematics or science. Instead, religious beliefs and rituals ought to renew our fundamental sense of mystery concerning the origin and meaning of existence.

This observation that religion—at its best—is associated with our sense of mystery and wonder resonated with the basic argument of one of my earlier books, *Religion and the Life Cycle*. I became curious whether fellow scholars in the field of the psychology of religion had

yet focused attention on the specific emotion of wonder. Imagine my surprise when I consulted the indexes of every psychology book in my personal library and couldn't find a single reference to wonder. When I turned to books specifically on the psychology of religion I was able to find some entries on awe and mystery, but again none on wonder! It became clear that a book on the connection between wonder and personal spirituality was well overdue.

A second conversation that sparked my interest in this topic took place during a debate I organized for students in Bradley University's Honors Program. The topic of the debate was "Can an educated person be religious?" At one point in the debate a student turned to my colleague, Tom Pucelik, and asked him whether being religious really made any difference in a person's life. Tom paused for a moment and then conceded that someone could go through life without being religious. Many good people do. Tom then added that you can also go through life without love or without art. But if you have ever been in love or been moved by great art, you know that they open up entirely new dimensions to your life. Sure, you can get through life without love or art, but your life wouldn't have the rich texture that only they can bring. The same, he said, is true of religion. I got to be thinking that this applies equally well to my basic point about the experience of wonder. You can surely get through life without a developed sense of wonder, but you would lack certain sensibilities that enrich the texture of human existence.

In many ways this book is a continuation of those conversations. It explores just how and why religion—at its best—holds us in a state of wonder. And although it concedes that you can surely go through life without a developed sense of wonder, it tries to show that a life shaped by wonder has rich textures that it would otherwise lack. A life shaped by wonder, as we shall see, is characterized by intellectual and moral sensibilities that open up the widest possible world of personal fulfillment.

ACKNOWLEDGMENTS

I HAD NEVER STUDIED EMOTION IN A SYSTEMATIC FASH-
ion prior to beginning this project. Imagine my sudden loss of
confidence when I realized that the word "wonder" couldn't be
found in the index of any of the first thirty psychology texts I consulted! If I had been left all to myself, this project would never have
moved forward.

The first to lend assistance was Kelly Bulkeley. Kelly, the author of
several excellent books that link modern dream research and humanistic inquiry, had just ventured on the topic of wonder, too. He
graciously sent me a copy of a paper he had delivered at an annual
meeting of the American Academy of Religion. His thoughts on the
topic were most helpful.

Two colleagues in Bradley University's Department of Psychology
took time to prepare bibliographical suggestions and clarify critical terms. Dave Schmitt, an evolutionary psychologist, steered me
toward works that examine the evolutionary-adaptive function of
emotions and alerted me to some of the theoretical land mines that
would await me. Derek Montgomery, a developmental psychologist,
responded to continuing queries on my part. His e-mail correspondence became a lively tutorial through which I learned a great deal
about the role of emotion in cognitive development.

John Corrigan, Edwin Scott Gaustad Professor of Religion at
Florida State University, was exceedingly generous with support
and guidance. His publications in the field of religion and emotion

steered me in profitable directions. His personal encouragement was even more appreciated.

Finally, a host of great colleagues at Bradley continue to make my professional work fun. Special thanks go to my dean, Claire Etaugh, who provides a role model for our college's dual commitment to teaching and research. Doug Crowe, Kevin Teeven, Kevin Stein, Dave Pardieck, Chuck Stoner, and Sam Fan help regenerate me when emotions lag. And our assistant vice president for university relations (my wife, Kathy) continues to be the wonder of my life.

WONDER

1. Introduction

Wonder is the feeling of the philosopher, and
philosophy begins in wonder.— SOCRATES

ALMOST EVERYONE I TALK TO THESE DAYS DESCRIBES HIM
or herself as spiritual. Yet few have a very clear idea of what
"being spiritual" really means. Most of us find it easier to
use the word as vaguely as possible. This way we can get credit for
being spiritual (which is assumed to be a good thing) without having
to commit ourselves to any fixed set of ideas or practices. The problem is that it has become difficult to know just what does and doesn't
count for spirituality anymore. Some flexibility in defining what
constitutes a spiritual outlook on life is surely appropriate. But this
shouldn't keep us from trying to understand what distinguishes a
spiritual approach to life from its secular counterpart. Nor should
our desire to respect individual differences in spirituality prevent us
from developing criteria with which we might judge whether "being
spiritual" really is such a good thing.

This book explores the experience of wonder and argues that it is
one of the defining elements of spirituality. My argument that wonder is a principal source of spirituality is both descriptive and normative. That is, I first draw on the natural and social sciences in order to
describe how the emotion of wonder elicits belief in the existence of a
more-than-physical reality. This descriptive part of my argument

includes an overview of the role that wonder plays in stimulating intellectual, moral, and aesthetic growth over the course of the human life span. My second task is normative, but in a psychological rather than either theological or ethical way. That is, I use fairly standard measures of psychological health to show that a life shaped by wonder is qualitatively "better" than a life that is relatively devoid of this emotion. Specifically, I argue that the intellectual, moral, and aesthetic characteristics linked to wonder transform personal life in ways that are, on balance, consistent with the highest levels of psychological development. I further wish to defend the view that wonder not only is but also should be a principal source of personal spirituality. Wonder excites our ontological imagination in ways that enhance our capacity to seek deeper patterns in the universe. A life shaped by wonder is thus more likely to steer a middle course between a purely secular life and a narrowly religious life. On the one hand, wonder prompts us to diverge from a purely secular outlook on life. It entices us to entertain the possibility that our highest fulfillment might require adapting ourselves to a metaphysical reality. Yet, on the other hand, wonder encourages an open-ended or heuristic approach to life. It thus imbues personal spirituality with a fresh quality, making it unlikely that we will reduce our basic belief in the existence of something "more" to narrow doctrines or creeds.

I am not attempting to reduce the whole of religion to the emotion of wonder. A wide variety of emotions play a role in personal religiosity. But if we define the word "spirituality" to mean a person's motivation to align his or her life with some kind of "higher" order of existence, I am suggesting that we will evidence a vital and psychologically mature form of spirituality in direct proportion to the presence of wonder in our lives.

Religion and the Emotions

The attempt to identify the emotional sources of religion goes back to antiquity. Our modern, Western views on the topic can be traced back to the writings of the Moravian theologian Friedrich

Schleiermacher (1764–1834). Born in a pietistic Christian community, Schleiermacher was among the first generation of Christian theologians to face the full brunt of the Enlightenment's attack on biblical faith. The Enlightenment was an era of unprecedented faith in reason. The scientific discoveries of Kepler, Brahe, and Newton proved that the mysteries of the universe can be reduced to a precise and lawful order. Educated people were confident that scientific discoveries such as these would continue to lift the veil of human ignorance. Religion, because it was associated with ancient biblical writings that had no scientific support, paled by comparison to the era's new intellectual outlook.

Schleiermacher was acutely aware of the cultural rift developing between science and religion. He realized, moreover, that culturally sophisticated people were unlikely to choose religion over science so long as religion was identified with backward ideas. Schleiermacher devised a strategy for defending religion that from the outset conceded that the "cultural despisers" of religion raised a number of valid criticisms. But, he contended, these criticisms missed the most important point about religion (Christianity). They attacked only the doctrines of religion and thus ignored the distinctive mode of human experience that gives rise to these doctrines. Schleiermacher was arguing that religion has its own unique "data"—the data of specifically religious emotions. Religion is different from all other areas of human existence in that it arises out of a unique mode of *feeling*. Schleiermacher consequently didn't view religion as a form of knowledge. Indeed, in his opinion the cultural difficulties that religion faced were largely due to mistakenly equating religion with formal doctrines that compete with other realms of knowledge such as science or mathematics.

Schleiermacher opened up an exciting new way of thinking about religion when he proposed that it originates in what he termed the "feeling of absolute dependence." Schleiermacher was thus arguing that religion is anchored in a very particular kind of feeling or emotion. It is possible that Schleiermacher's reference to "feeling" (*das gefuhl*) is not precisely what modern social science considers an emo-

tion per se. He was, after all, trying to draw attention to the subjective feeling that accompanies an intuitive grasp or consciousness of relationship to God. Yet because Schleiermacher viewed this "immediate feeling" as something that arises in response or relationship to something other than the self, it seems to constitute an emotional state. Religion, he contended, was the subjectively experienced "sense and taste for the infinite."[1] Experiences of truth, goodness, and beauty stir in us a feeling that points us to what is absolute in life: "To seek and to find this infinite and eternal factor in all that lives and moves, in all growth and change, in all action and passion, and to have and to know life itself only in immediate feeling—that is religion."[2]

Schleiermacher's equation of religion with a particular mode of personal feeling has greatly influenced both liberal Christian theology and the academic study of religion. Rudolf Otto (1869–1937), for example, equated religion with the emotions engendered by an encounter with the holy. In his famous study of religion titled *The Idea of the Holy*, Otto maintained that religion originates in our apprehension of "the wholly other." That is, religion is distinguished from other areas of life in that it rests in the qualitatively distinct feeling that one has encountered something that wholly transcends the material world. According to Otto, this "other" is experienced as awesome, numinous, mysterious, and beyond our control. An experiential encounter with the "the wholly other" evokes feelings of reverence, submission, dependence, rapture, and exaltation. An analysis of these emotions "shows that above and beyond our rational being lies hidden the ultimate and highest part of our nature, which can find no satisfaction in the mere allaying of the needs of our sensuous, psychical, or intellectual impulses and cravings."[3] In Otto's view these emotions engendered by an encounter with the holy form the experiential core of religion; doctrines are secondary but "obscure and inadequate symbols" of the encounter itself.

Schleiermacher and Otto illustrate the kinds of theological and academic arguments used to identify those feelings or emotions that are unique to religion. Not all such arguments have been used to defend religion from its modern critics, however. Sigmund Freud

(1856–1939) was undoubtedly the most eloquent of those who realized that this connection between religion and emotion can also be used to demonstrate that religion is a backward, retrogressive force within human nature. Freud developed two distinct but interconnected arguments that attacked religion precisely because it was linked with emotions rather than with reason. Both arguments associated religion with specific emotions he deemed inimical to the full development of humanity's potential for rational self-control. Freud links religion with feelings of helplessness, dependency, and fear. Life, he notes, is harsh. Humans are everywhere faced with such terrifying realities as disease, natural disasters, and impending death. These dangers prompt even grown adults to wish for a father figure to deliver them from evil. Our fundamental helplessness causes us to yearn for a supernatural protector. Religion, then, consists of the wishful thinking born of human helplessness, dependency, and fear. But, Freud cautioned, these wishes are illusory. Religious beliefs amount to nothing more than superstition and irrational wishes. The emotions that lead us to adopt them ultimately stand in the way of the development of a strong, rational outlook on life. Yes, religion is linked with particular emotions, but it is in humanity's highest interest to suppress these emotions and replace them with clear, problem-solving rationality.

Freud also linked religion with the emotion of guilt. A medical physician trained in an era greatly influenced by evolutionary biology, Freud understandably emphasized the role of instincts in controlling our thought and behavior. He assumed that our strongest instincts, such as sex and aggression, are antisocial in that they impel us to seek personal satisfaction rather than to conform to social protocol. Every culture needs to find ways to induce people to repress their antisocial desires and instead to obey conventional ethical standards. Most cultures do this through religion and its beliefs concerning divine judgment. Religious beliefs concerning the afterlife and a judgmental God create in us a sense of guilt whenever we break society's moral code. As Freud put it, "the price we pay for our advance in civilization is a loss of happiness through the heightening

of the sense of guilt."[4] Religion is culture's mechanism for producing guilt and then using this guilt to coerce us into conforming to our society's moral code. Religion controls people by taking advantage of their emotional vulnerability. Freud was himself a moralist and fully recognized the importance of cultural institutions that can help humanity attain civility through the control of its antisocial impulses. Freud's difficulty with religion wasn't that it seeks to redirect our instinctual passion but that it does so on the basis of ancient superstitions that haven't kept pace with cultural progress. He argued that humanity cannot take the next step forward in its cultural evolution until it once and for all abandons the illusions of religion for a more scientific view of the world.

Thus, while Schleiermacher and Otto identified the emotional roots of religion as a means of defending religion, Freud pointed to the emotional core of religion as a means of demonstrating that religion is inherently false and manipulative. Scholars continue to argue both sides of this issue even to this day. Religious historian John Corrigan has written an essay that summarizes the history and present status of the study of religion and emotion.[5] Corrigan observes that in addition to identifying the emotional sources of religiosity, scholars have studied the way that religion seeks to pattern or control emotional expression among its followers. The latter constitutes what Peter Stearns and Carol Stearns have called "emotionology," the study of the "collective emotional standards of a society."[6] Corrigan notes that a substantial portion of the scholarship in this field has concentrated on the emotions of anger, fear, bliss, love, shame/guilt, hatred, mourning, jealousy, melancholy, and even humor. Hatred, for example, is often a principal element in apocalyptic religion, as belief in an end-times enemy often vents hostility toward those who don't belong to one's own religious clan.[7] Love, on the other hand, is also historically associated with religion. This is particularly the case in the highly rapturous love of God found both in the Hindu devotional movement of bhakti and in Christian mystical traditions.[8] We might finally note that a large number of studies have also assessed the experience of joy or bliss in various mystical

traditions. Bliss is, for example, associated with Hindu meditational systems that help people overcome duality of thought and experience and find union with God.[9]

There has, then, been a great deal of historical scholarship that has explored the emotional component of religious life in a wide assortment of chronological and geographical settings. Yet, as John Corrigan notes, sorely needed are "works that engage the very issue of the definition of emotion in religion."[10] Among other things, this will require utilizing insights on the nature and function of emotion that have gained widespread support in both the natural and social sciences. The natural and social sciences have generated theoretical perspectives for understanding emotions that can help us address a number of new and interesting questions: How and why did those emotions most associated with religion first emerge in humanity's evolutionary history? What affect do various emotions have on an individual's cognitive development? Do religiously charged emotions contribute to—or impair—humanity's adaptation to the natural and social environments? How do religious institutions develop beliefs and rituals that lead to the cultivation or concealment of specific emotional states? Are there empirically grounded criteria that might be used to help us discriminate between those emotions that best engender mature spirituality and those emotions that stifle the full expression of our spiritual potentials?

Recent decades have witnessed important advances in the study of emotions in a wide variety of academic fields (i.e., evolutionary biology, evolutionary psychology, developmental psychology, and philosophy). The following chapters review these advances for understanding not only emotion as a general category but also the specific emotion of wonder. This book is a pioneering effort in two important ways. First, it will make an important contribution to the modern study of emotion in that it examines wonder using the impressive advances in emotion research in the biological sciences, the social and behavioral sciences, philosophy, and cultural history over the past few decades. It does so, moreover, by striving to retain contact with the lived experience of wonder. Continued attention to the

biographical context of specific instances of wonder provides a helpful safeguard against the academic tendency to reify one of the most slippery and variable of all human experiences. Second, this is the first book-length study of the connection between wonder and religion. Such a study requires exploring somewhat uncharted territory, but the intellectual rewards seem more than worth the intellectual risk. The specific emotions identified in previous studies (e.g., anger, fear, bliss, love, shame/guilt, hatred, mourning, jealousy, and melancholy) reveal much about religion, but they certainly don't tell the whole story. Because experiences of wonder are unique in their ability to lure us into extended engagement with that which lies beyond the limits of rational comprehension, they hold great promise for helping us understand the dynamics of personal spirituality.

Emotion, Wonder, and Religion

The *Oxford English Dictionary* defines wonder as "the emotion excited by the perception of something novel and unexpected." It continues by further defining wonder as "astonishment mingled with perplexity or bewildered curiosity." Although many kinds of "novel and unexpected" phenomena can elicit our sense of wonder, it often accompanies our perception of something that strikes us as intensely powerful, real, true, and/or beautiful.[11]

As the OED suggests, there is a close connection between wonder and curiosity. Both are responses to seemingly inexplicable phenomena. We might, however, distinguish between wonder and curiosity in two important ways. First, we typically associate curiosity with active attempts to understand, and even manipulate, apparently anomalous features of the environment. In contrast, the emotion of wonder is more passive; it usually leads to cognitive reflection about the meaning of unexpected perceptions rather than to active exploration. Second, curiosity is associated with analysis. Curiosity entails efforts to understand events or objects by breaking them down into their component parts. Wonder, on the other hand, is the experience of contemplating how the various parts relate to a greater (even if

unobserved) whole. Wonder prompts us to consider how particularly vivid displays of vitality, beauty, or power might reveal a purpose or intentionality of the universe as a whole. As such, wonder stimulates efforts to discern what is of intrinsic value or meaning (as opposed to what is of utilitarian value or meaning). And it consequently elicits efforts to find a harmonious relationship with, rather than active mastery of, our wider surroundings.

Even though it is a common human emotion, wonder is rarely a topic of scientific study. A recent overview of Western scientific opinion on the subject of emotion found that researchers disagree about the exact number of human emotions. In part this debate involves the distinction between primary and secondary emotions. Primary emotions are those that exist at birth, as opposed to secondary emotions, which emerge over time (largely owing to social learning or as combinations and permutations of the primary emotions). This overview notes that virtually all theorists recognize fear, anger, and sadness as primary emotions and that there is near consensus on joy, love, and surprise.[12] Among the most frequently mentioned others are disgust, anticipation, ecstasy, adoration, interest, amazement, pensiveness, distraction, and grief. Some theorists have specifically mentioned that wonder has important affinities with interest, amazement, surprise, and joy. But not one major Western theorist in the past hundred years has explicitly listed wonder as one of the principal primary or secondary emotions.

This omission of wonder in Western scientific thought is especially odd in that other epochs and other cultures have recognized wonder as a principal human emotion. The seventeenth-century philosopher René Descartes listed wonder as one of the six principal emotions (along with desire, joy, love, hatred, and sadness). Descartes reasoned that emotions occur in the thinking part of ourselves, what he called the soul. Wonder, he claimed, is the first of the passions. He explained that "when a first encounter with an object surprises us and we judge it to be new, or very different from what we have hitherto known or from what we have supposed it ought to be, this causes us to wonder and to be surprised. And since this can

happen prior to our knowing at all whether this object is or is not serviceable to us, it seems that wonder is the first [i.e., in the sense of being the first to be awakened] of all the passions."[13]

Descartes explained that "wonder alone has the function of leading us to take note of those [features of experience] which appear only rarely."[14] He further opined that "only the dull and stupid are in no wise naturally disposed to wonder." Descartes cautioned, however, that wonder carries with it the inherent danger of making us intellectually passive. He believed that insofar as wonder prompts us to take interest in the extraordinary and mysterious in their own right, it potentially weakens our motivation for pursuing things "which might more usefully be studied." Those who are especially prone to wonder tend to be shy about applying their intellectual powers to the practical affairs of life.

As early as the third century B.C.E., an Indian text listed wonder as one of the nine principal human emotions. This treatise, the *Natyashastra*, is a canonical Sanskrit text investigating the nature of consciousness (particularly the effect that drama and other aesthetic experiences have in producing insight or revelatory changes in consciousness). Indian intellectuals labored diligently to develop an aesthetic theory that categorized the various emotional responses to theater and literature. The purpose was to understand how such art forms might invoke these emotional responses and elicit an experience of Brahman (the ultimate power of the universe that is immanent in all of existence). The sixth chapter of the *Natyashastra* distills centuries of thought on this topic by enumerating the nine basic emotions: sexual passion, amusement, sorrow, anger, fear, perseverance, disgust, serenity, and wonder.[15] It should be noted that the Indian notion of wonder has always differed from contemporary North American understandings of either "curiosity" or "surprise." It means something more than just being surprised or startled by the sudden perception of some unexpected event. Instead, wonder in the Indic tradition is a reaction to the opportunity to witness divine, heavenly, or exalted phenomena.[16] Wonder, therefore, is intimately linked with what the Indic tradition calls *darshan*, the ritual act of

seeing divinity. Whether occasioned by a temple icon or a sacred place in nature, "religious seeing" is thought to disclose the life and consciousness that pulsates throughout the whole of creation.[17] Traditional Hindu theology maintains that God, or absolute consciousness, is immanent in all things. For this reason, the act of "seeing" the divine is believed to overcome the usual division between experiencing subject and experienced object. Religious seeing entails actually participating in the essence and nature of the person or object that elicited this perception (including participating in the essence and nature of the divine ground of this person or object). Religious seeing is thus fraught with wonder. It takes a person beyond his or her own individuality to participate in a greater ontological whole.

The very attributes that make wonder stand out as a principal human emotion in the tradition out of which modern Hinduism has arisen probably account for why wonder has been largely neglected within Western science. Both biologists and psychologists bring an evolutionary paradigm to their study of emotions. As a consequence, they tend to emphasize those emotions that lead to the performance of adaptive behaviors such as withdrawal, avoidance, mating, or aggression. It is relatively rare for biologists and psychologists to study emotions that have no immediate survival value. Wonder, curiosity, and interest would be prime examples of emotions that lead to sustained attention to one's surroundings. All three motivate thought, perception, and action in ways that enable organisms to develop new and more creative modes of interaction with their environment. They are all adaptive, but in a less obvious and more long-term way. Researchers also tend to ignore wonder because of its propensity to prompt humans to contemplate nonphysical features of the universe (mistakenly leading some researchers to conclude that wonder is a misapplication of the brain's cognitive abilities).

This effort to draw on modern scientific literature in order to develop a multidisciplinary understanding of wonder is thus a pioneering one. Fortunately, several researchers have studied closely related emotional experiences and have noted their relevance for an understanding of wonder. For example, the highly regarded psychol-

ogists Carroll Izard and Brian Ackerman have analyzed the role of interest in regulating human behavior. Their account of interest begins by noting that it overlaps with other human traits such as "curiosity," "urge to explore or discover," "intrinsic motivation," and—importantly—"wonder." They explain that what makes the emotion of interest so fascinating is how it "animates and enlivens the mind and body. Interest provides the motivation and resources for constructive and creative endeavor, the development of intelligence, and personal growth." It "motivates exploration and learning, and guarantees the person's engagement in the environment. Survival and adaptation require such engagement. Interest supports creativity because it immerses one in the object or task and cues a sense of possibility. . . . Interest is the only emotion that can sustain long-term constructive or creative endeavors."[18]

As Izard and Ackerman note, wonder is similar to interest in its ability to animate and enliven the mind. Wonder, like heightened interest, momentarily suspends habitual ways of looking at the world and instead lures people into new and creative engagement with their surroundings. Rather than encouraging behaviors that distance us from our environment, wonder induces receptivity and openness. It prompts us to become more connected with the wider environment. Thus, even though wonder does not elicit aggression or defensive maneuvering, it has adaptive significance. In fact, the role of wonder in our lives alerts us to a broader understanding of adaptation. Adaptation requires receptivity as well as activity, creative ways of sensing one's connectedness with the world as well as ways of establishing a safe distance from potential danger. Even relatively passive emotional states such as wonder can contribute to our long-term adaptation. Wonder prompts us to consider life from new perspectives. It helps us get in touch with the unitary and relational aspects of reality. In this way wonder gives us a vision of our relatedness to the world, to other human beings, and to the ultimate source from which existence emerges.[19]

Wonder's capacity to stimulate novel engagement with the world can also be traced over the course of psychological growth from

infancy through adulthood. Each successive stage of psychological development presents us with new physical and social challenges. Mastering these challenges requires the gradual acquisition of new and increasingly complex cognitive skills. Emotions have a great influence over both the rate and precise nature of this developmental pattern. The noted cognitive theorist Jean Piaget, for example, identified curiosity as the key factor motivating our acquisition of cognitive skills. Piaget often used the metaphor of "little scientists" to capture the way that curiosity drives children to investigate and create in the context of their interactions with the world. Piaget's research confirmed that curiosity is rewarding in its own right, drawing children into sustained rapport with their environment and prompting them not just to register experience passively but to interpret such experience.

Implicit—but relatively neglected—in Piaget's work is the realization that we are also motivated to learn how to make connections between different kinds of things or to connect things in higher-order ways. Cognitive growth also requires our ability to entertain abstract or hypothetical constructions of reality. The existence of such higher-order conceptions of reality frees us from sheer necessity and brute survival to consider what our existential and ethical response to life might optimally be. Just as curiosity propels children to sustain their inquiries into the causal workings of physical reality, wonder is a prime motivating factor in the acquisition of higher-order conceptions of reality. The experience of wonder is characterized by the disruption of previous cognitive schemata. Wonder, then, is an emotional experience that invites us to entertain belief in the existence and causal activity of an order of reality that lies beyond or behind sensory appearances. It is therefore possible to argue that wonder is indispensable to the development of humanity's full cognitive potential.

The ability to conceptualize a more-than-physical order of reality is absolutely necessary if we are to attain a variety of distinctively human cognitive skills. This would be true, for example, of the ability to formulate religious or metaphysical conceptions of the universe. It

would be equally true of our ability to formulate conceptions of morality and justice. Indeed, moral theorist Martha Nussbaum concludes that wonder is the principal emotion that can lift us beyond the pursuit of immediate self-interest.[20] Nussbaum notes how wonder takes us beyond self-absorption and makes it possible for us to see people and objects as worthy in their own right. Wonder is thus intimately linked with compassion and the capacity to act to preserve the integrity of life even when there is no immediate connection with one's own self-interest.

Wonder is, furthermore, intimately linked with humanity's propensity to take a religious, as distinct from scientific or commonsensical, stance toward life. The highly regarded philosopher and psychologist William James once summarized human religiosity as "the belief that there is an unseen order, and that our supreme good lies in harmoniously adjusting ourselves thereto."[21] James expanded on this characterization of religion by suggesting that humans are prone to granting ontological reality to an order of existence that somehow lies beyond the range of our physical senses. It is, James observes, "as if there were in the human consciousness a *sense of reality, a feeling of objective presence, a perception* of what we may call 'something there,' . . . a sense of present reality more diffused and general than that which our special senses yield."[22] Of all human emotions, wonder is surely the most responsible for prompting such belief in the existence of "an unseen order." Wonder originates in response to novel or unexpected stimuli. What distinguishes the experience of wonder, however, is that it motivates us to contemplate the possibility that there are causal powers existing "beyond" our immediate physical surroundings. In other words, wonder encourages belief in a metaphysical order of existence—an order, moreover, that has causal relevance to our lives. Wonder is for this reason the emotion most closely associated with humanity's spiritual impulses.

The close connection between wonder and spirituality alerts us to the diverse array of human activities that might potentially prompt glimpses of an "unseen order" of life. The rituals and forms of worship orchestrated by our formal religious institutions are, at their

best, time-tested means for holding us in a state of wonder. Yet we find equally vivid instances of wondrous emotions in activities that have no connection with organized religion. Music, art, love, scientific investigation, and feelings of rapport with nature are all known to elicit profound emotions of wonder. And all are known to engender profound personal transformations. They invigorate us. They help us abandon dysfunctional identities and take a fresh approach to life. They help us feel free of environmental conditioning and capable of creative self-direction. And, importantly, they help us feel in touch with issues of cosmic import.

Any number of commonly recurring experiences are capable of eliciting the emotion of wonder. This is particularly the case when vivid instances of vitality, beauty, and truth prompt us to wonder. Such encounters prompt us to suspend our utilitarian calculations and delight in a nonegoistic contemplation of the causal power that might make such vitality, beauty, and truth possible. Wonder entices us to consider the reality of the unseen, the existence of a more general order of existence from which this world derives its meaning and purpose. It is thus only to be expected that wonder also entices us to believe that our supreme good lies in harmoniously adjusting ourselves thereto. Wonder, it would seem, is one of the principal sources of humanity's spiritual impulse. A life shaped by wonder might, therefore, be a defining example of what "being spiritual" means at its very best.

2. Emotion and Evolution

Wonder is what sets us apart from other life forms.
No other species wonders about the meaning of existence
or the complexity of the universe or themselves.
—HERBERT W. BOYER, co-founder of Genentech, Inc.

THE MODERN SCIENTIFIC STUDY OF THE EMOTIONS CAN be traced to Charles Darwin. Thirteen years after publishing his epochal *On the Origin of Species* (1859), Darwin produced a volume titled *The Expression of the Emotions in Man and Animals*. This study was not a thorough analysis of emotions per se. It was, rather, a more limited attempt to account for why we continue to exhibit certain emotional expressions even though they no longer appear to serve adaptive functions. Yet *The Expression of the Emotions* remains a classic in the study of emotions both because it exemplifies Darwin's distinctive manner of analyzing biological phenomena and because it explains how discrete emotional expressions affect the chances of survival.

Like other natural scientists, Darwin was interested in matters of what, how, and when.[1] That is, Darwin investigated issues such as what each emotion expresses, how these expressions are physiologically produced, and when these expressions occur. But Darwin's most important contribution to the study of the emotions is his answer to the more important question of why we have emotions at all.

Darwin set out to explore why animals display their emotions through expressive behaviors such as facial expressions, gestures, and postures.[2] He utilized data from his own fieldwork as well as observations provided by zookeepers, explorers, and missionaries who had lived in nonliterate human cultures. Darwin began by examining, arranging, and classifying these data. He then proposed three principles that he believed could account for the origin and function of emotions in our evolutionary history. The first principle had to do with the functional value of emotions. Darwin described this as "the principle of serviceable associated habits." By this he meant that emotional states are of functional value to the individual. Emotions facilitate behavior that bring individual gratification and promote survival. In his words, "certain complex actions are of direct or indirect service under certain states of the mind."[3] The second principle was what Darwin called "the principle of antithesis." He explained that "there is a strong and involuntary tendency to the performance of movements directly opposite of others."[4] Expressive behaviors signal our intentions to others. Thus, for example, we shrug our shoulders when we feel helpless because it is the opposite of the movements we make when we are asserting ourselves aggressively.

The third principle concerning the evolutionary origin of the emotions had to do with the direct action of the nervous system (over and beyond conscious intention or acquired habit). Darwin's point here is that our emotions are part of our basic physiology. We sweat, tremble, faint, or even smile as a result of direct actions of the nervous system. These emotional expressions are therefore innate and biologically grounded. Emotions are inherited traits preserved through natural selection because they contributed to the survival of the species. Yet, Darwin observed in *The Expression of the Emotions*, the emotional expressions that humans have inherited are patterns of action that occur even "though they may not . . . be of the least use" in our current day.[5] His point was that many emotional expressions we find in humans and animals today exist because they were functional in our evolutionary past even though they may no longer be of any

use. Therefore some emotion-based expressions persist not because they are useful in our present settings but because they are triggered by environmental cues similar to those that had elicited them in our evolutionary past.

Darwin's overall answer to the question of why humans (and other animals) have emotions was thus a functional one. He showed that emotional expressions—at least as they initially emerged in our evolutionary history—facilitate adaptation and survival. He pointed out, for example, that the emotions of fear and anger often promote survival by triggering behaviors that make an animal appear much bigger than it really is. Darwin observed, "Hardly any expressive movement is so general as the involuntary erection of the hairs, feathers and other dermal appendages. . . . These appendages were erected under the excitement of anger or terror: more especially when these emotions are combined, or quickly succeed each other. The action serves to make the animal appear larger and more fright-ful to its enemies or rivals, and is generally accompanied by various voluntary movements adapted for the same purpose, and by the utterance of savage sounds."[6]

For Darwin, then, emotional expressions were originally pre-served through the process of natural selection because they affect our chances of survival. They mobilize us for action. They communi-cate information about our intentions. In short, emotions contrib-ute to our overall biological fitness, which can be defined in terms of our ability to survive, procreate, and raise offspring to the point of biological viability.

Darwin's contributions to the study of emotions were largely overlooked during the first half of the twentieth century. The aca-demic world became increasingly interested in the role of culture in determining human behavior. The discipline of cultural anthropol-ogy, for example, gained enormous prestige in this era by demon-strating the vast influence that cultural conditioning has on human beings. Cultural anthropologists typically assert that the origin and communicative functions of emotions can be explained almost en-tirely by reference to social patterns of interaction.

A very similar point of view became dominant among academic psychologists during the middle decades of the twentieth century. The behaviorist model popularized by John B. Watson and B. F. Skinner maintained that all human behavior is conditioned by the environment. Emotion is no exception. Skinner argued that emotion is essentially a covert behavior.[7] What we call emotions are simply internal behaviors that have been conditioned by the environment. Emotions are the feeling states that have been learned through both respondent and operant conditioning. It was important to Skinner that we understand that emotions are not inner causes of behavior. Thus, for example, a person might feel angry and then strike someone. But Skinner's view is that "anger" per se did not cause the hitting behavior. Both the inner emotion of "anger" and the hitting gestures are learned behaviors. Aversive stimuli often elicit inner responses. For such a response to become "anger," however, these stimuli must be interpreted and labeled with the vocabulary reinforced by our family and other members of our social community. If the hitting behavior is reinforced, then the whole sequence of inner emotional response and overt emotional behavior is conditioned and will repeat itself when similar stimuli present themselves. In sum, the behaviorist school of psychological thought directed attention away from viewing emotions as either biological or universal. Instead it popularized the view that emotions are patterns of covert behaviors that can be fully explained with reference to environmental conditioning.

The field of social psychology was yet another academic discipline that emphasized the cultural (rather than biological) nature of emotions. The basic theoretical assumption underlying social psychology is that human thought and behavior are profoundly influenced by a web of interpersonal influences. The "interpersonal influence" model was applied to the study of emotions in a famous study by Stanley Schachter and Jerome Singer in 1962.[8] They hypothesized that emotions consist of a state of physiological arousal paired with a specific cognitive label or evaluation. In their view some event creates physiological arousal, which individuals then need to interpret or

label. The specific emotion that a person experiences thus depends not on the physiological arousal per se but rather on the cognitive evaluation he or she uses to label or interpret the arousal. Thus, for example, the same physiological arousal may be experienced as either eagerness or fear depending on the cognitive labels the person attaches to it.

Schachter and Singer tested this hypothesis by injecting epinephrine into three groups of experimental subjects and a placebo into a fourth group. They provided the experimental subjects with differing explanations of what side effects to expect from the injected drugs. Some subjects received accurate explanations, others inaccurate explanations, and still others no explanation whatsoever. One member of each group was in collusion with Schachter and Singer. This experimental plant was instructed to act in specific ways, giving experimental subjects a role model from whom they might take cues about what effects to expect from the drug. One plant modeled euphoric actions in front of all the misinformed subjects and half of all other subjects. Another plant modeled angry actions in front of the remaining subjects. Schachter and Singer's basic finding (though the data varied considerably between the "euphoric" modeling and "angry" modeling) was that those who were misinformed or not informed at all were more likely to imitate the plant's mood and behavior. Their study seemed to confirm two basic points about emotions. The first is that emotions are largely created by the cognitive label people add to their state of physiological arousal. The second is that this cognitive label is largely garnered from social references. It should be pointed out that a number of other investigators have criticized the experimental methods used by Schachter and Singer and have argued that their findings have not been replicated in similar studies. Yet Schachter and Singer's study was widely cited and succeeded in drawing attention to the importance of nonbiological factors in structuring human emotions.

These trends within the social sciences were matched by the emergence of the "constructivist" position in humanities disciplines such as philosophy, history, and religious studies. The constructivist posi-

tion rejects biological accounts of human behavior and is suspicious of efforts to find universals in human nature. This school of thought argues instead that human behavior and even "inner experiences" (including our emotions or even mystical experience) are "constructed" by culture. In this view distinct emotions are the product of distinct cultural conditions and are thus not reducible to some kind of universal biological principle.[9] Rom Harré and others contend that those who argue for a physiological basis to the emotions are mistakenly perpetuating belief in an "ontological illusion."[10] Harré maintains that if we want to study an emotional phenomenon such as anger we should not ask what anger is but rather how the word "anger" is actually used in specific cultural contexts. He suggests, for example, that the "the study of emotions like envy (and jealousy) will require careful attention to the details of local systems of rights and obligations, of criteria of value and so on. In short, these emotions cannot seriously be studied without attention to the local moral order."[11]

Academic trends thus had a profound influence on how the emotions were regarded in twentieth-century academic thought. As a consequence, many scholars in the humanities and social sciences came to regard emotions as socially programmed behaviors with little biological or psychological basis. This trend began to reverse, however, in the 1980s. Both biologists and psychologists have become more interested in the biological factors that influence human thought and action. The field of genetics has established that there are strong biological influences on almost every form of human behavior. Meanwhile, evolutionary biology spawned two new academic disciplines, evolutionary psychology and sociobiology. Both disciplines brought new perspectives to bear on a variety of human traits, including emotions. Evolutionary psychology extended Darwin's "why" questions to the study of mental activities. The main task of evolutionary psychology has been to explain why natural selection favored the kinds of mental activity that we discern in organisms today. The field of sociobiology is similarly concerned with why humans and other social organisms evolved particular behavior pat-

terns. Sociobiologists, too, assume that the behavior of social organisms can be fully explained with reference to the process of natural selection.

These and related disciplines have greatly expanded our framework for understanding the origin and function of humanity's emotional life. As a result, most contemporary researchers have adopted a theoretical model that recognizes both genetic and cultural factors in the expression of human emotion. Most researchers would agree with Richard LeDoux, who concludes that emotions are "biological functions of the nervous system." According to LeDoux, there is compelling evidence that our genes give us the raw materials out of which to build our emotions.

> [Our genes] specify the kind of nervous system we will have, the kinds of mental processes in which it can engage, and the kinds of bodily functions it can control. But the exact way we act, think, and feel in a particular situation is determined by many other factors and is not predestined in our genes. Some, if not many, emotions do have a biological basis, but social, which is to say cognitive, factors are also crucially important. Nature and nurture are partners in our emotional life. The trick is to figure what their unique contributions are.[12]

That the experience of wonder has a biological base there can be no doubt. But determining just what the unique contributions of nature and nurture are in constructing such experiences is indeed tricky business.

Emotions in Biological Context

The resurgence of interest in the evolutionary and genetic basis of human behavior brought with it a new interest in the study of human emotions. Evolutionary theory assumes that the natural environment creates survival problems that must be successfully solved if organisms are to survive and produce viable offspring.[13] These sur-

vival problems come in a variety of forms. Some are largely bio-chemical in nature; organisms must efficiently metabolize food and fight off infections or parasites. Other survival problems have to do with self-defense and self-preservation; organisms must make appropriate responses to predators and prey. Still other survival problems are more properly social in nature; organisms must make appropriate responses to caregivers and care solicitors as well behave in ways that minimize intragroup discord.

Biological evolution has shaped each species' ability to adapt to environmental challenges through the interplay of two independent variables: genetic mutation and natural selection. When genes replicate, there is always the slight chance of variation. Genetic mutations are accidental. They occur randomly and with no direct relationship to the process of natural selection. Most changes in an organism's genetic code are detrimental and lead to that organism's death. In other words, nature "selects against" these new genetic patterns. Other genetic mutations have little or no effect on an organism's chances for survival and are thus "neutral" from an evolutionary point of view. Occasionally, however, a genetic mutation leads to biochemical, anatomical, or behavioral changes that greatly increase an organism's biological fitness. In these cases nature eventually "selects for" these changes, and they become part of that species' genetically determined adaptive strengths.

From the perspective of evolutionary theory our entire neurological and visceral systems were designed by natural selection to solve the adaptive problems confronted by our biological ancestors. This includes our emotional system. As evolutionary psychologists Leda Cosmides and John Tooby note, emotions can be regarded as "super-ordinate programs" that regulate behavior so that we can successfully address the adaptive problems specific to the human species.[14] Persistent environmental challenges selected for genetic changes that ensure proper adaptive responses. Cosmides and Tooby refer to such persistent environmental challenges as "evolutionarily recurrent situations," by which they mean "a cluster of repeated proba-

bilistic relationships among events, conditions, actions, and choice consequences that endured over a sufficient stretch of evolutionary time to have had selective consequences on the design of the mind, and that were probabilistically associated with cues detectable by humans."[15]

Natural selection favored emotion programs capable of negotiating such recurring situations. It follows that emotion programs are biologically grounded patterns of adaptive response. Their purpose is to regulate cognition and behavior such that we can successfully master the many requirements of biological survival (e.g., cooperation, sexual attraction, coalitional aggression, incest avoidance, predator avoidance, investigative scanning of the environment).

From the viewpoint of evolutionary theory, then, emotions may be conceptualized as superordinate programs that govern adaptive behavior. They serve adaptation by mobilizing and coordinating a host of perceptual, cognitive, and behavioral subprograms. This biological perspective on human behavior thus views emotions as having causal influence over such adaptive activities as directing attention, selectively activating memory, guiding cognitive inference, creating motivational priorities, and communicating intention.

Emotions as Motivational Systems

The emergence of an evolutionary-adaptive framework for understanding emotions has by no means ended disputes among scientific researchers. Debates still rage over fundamental issues entailed in defining precisely what an emotion is. How, for example, does an emotion differ from a feeling or a mood? Which, if any, emotions are innate (i.e., biological, genetically governed, and universal across cultures) and which are learned (i.e., produced by social and cultural forces)? How many emotions are there—and what criteria might distinguish between distinct emotions and feeling states composed of one or more of these distinct emotions?

The complexity of the scholarly debates over the nature of emo-

tions recently prompted Aaron Ben-Ze'ev to conclude that "the nature, causes, and consequences of the emotions are among the least understood aspects of human experience."[16] Ben-Ze'ev suggests that it is the "subtlety of the emotions" that makes them so difficult to reduce to any single scientific framework. Emotions, after all, vary according to personal and contextual circumstances. Furthermore, our understanding of brain physiology is still too inadequate to shed definitive light on the complexities and subtleties of the emotions. We are, for example, a long way from truly knowing whether the feeling states we call emotions cause neurophysiological changes or, instead, are simply the feeling states that accompany these changes. Furthermore, research in the area of emotions depends heavily on subjects' facial expressions, bodily gestures, and verbal reports—all of which permit multiple interpretations.

While there may not be total unanimity in the contemporary scientific study of emotions, there does appear to be considerable consensus. Most researchers today approach human nature from an evolutionary-adaptive perspective. For this reason they tend to view emotions as part of complex, circular feedback systems that connect people with their environment.[17] It is assumed that stimulus events, either environmental or physiological, trigger an emotional program whose purpose is to mobilize the organism for an appropriate response to this stimulus. Richard Lazarus and Robert Plutchik are among those who argue that cognition is always entailed in, and actually precedes, human emotion. By this they mean that even in infancy humans begin to interpret sensory stimuli. Lazarus, for example, argued that emotions involve our appraisals of the environment, our relationships with others, and our attempts at coping with these relationships. Lazarus's notion of the role of appraisal in human emotions is meant to draw attention to the process through which we continually evaluate (often unconsciously) the potential harms and benefits existing in each interaction with the environment.[18] Unexpected or uncertain perceptions are the most likely to arouse emotions. The brain's emotion programs are triggered by

such discrepancies between expectations drawn from past experiences and signals from the present environment. Their goal is to mobilize the organism for appropriate response.

One of the foremost authorities on emotion, psychologist Carroll Izard, notes that because emotions mobilize us for action they "constitute the primary motivational system for human beings."[19] Emotions arouse and coordinate neural programs that direct behavior. Research has established the role of emotions in a wide variety of neural programs involved with cognition and behavior. Leda Cosmides and John Tooby, for example, conclude that there is sufficient evidence to show that emotions redirect such vital activities as goal setting, information gathering, selective perception, utilization of goal-specific conceptual frameworks, activation of goal-specific memory, structuring of attention, regulation of physiological processes, communication of intention, and shifts in energy level.[20] Because emotions direct what we are interested in and prioritize our goals, they also influence our perception and cognition. They prompt us to scan our environment and to focus attention selectively on data that appear relevant to our survival and mobilized interests. Emotions also send out distinct patterns of instructions to organ systems, muscle groups, or various metabolic processes—thereby readying the organism for specific kinds of action. It should be noted, too, that many emotions produce species-typical gestures or expressions (e.g., facial expressions, drooping of the shoulders, raising hair) that broadcast our behavioral intentions to others. Such emotionally expressive communication is a means by which different species survive and achieve both individual and communal goals.

The Nature and Variety of Emotions

The debate whether emotions are innate (biological) rather than the product of social and cultural forces continues to divide researchers in the field. There is, however, strong consensus that emotions are biologically grounded (innate and genetic) even if from birth on they

come, to varying degrees, under the control of cultural influences. Both Paul Ekman's and Carroll Izard's studies of how emotions are communicated through facial expression have been embraced as having corroborated the argument that emotions are genetically based.[21] Their cross-cultural studies of facial expressions indicate that many emotional expressions are both generated and recognized reliably by humans everywhere they have been tested. And, insofar as emotions are human universals, it would also seem likely that they have a firm genetic basis.

There are those who continue to challenge the biological basis of emotion. As mentioned earlier in this chapter, Rom Harré is among those who argue for the social or cultural origins of emotional behavior. Harré's position might be considered a strong version of what is called constructivism (i.e., the view that all human thought and knowledge are constructed through specific social and cultural activities). Strong versions of constructivism assert that human nature is almost completely shaped by social—not biological—factors. Strong constructivist positions deny the existence of universal or biologically based components of human nature. Moreover, this position is highly suspicious of all knowledge claims (especially those of modern science), since it holds that all human thought is radically determined by historical and social forces. A major weakness of this school of thought is that it is exceedingly doctrinaire. It dismisses most arguments from the natural and social sciences out of hand without engaging them in ways that make mutually informing discussions possible. A truly interdisciplinary approach to the human emotions, then, is not possible on the basis of strong versions of the constructivist outlook (any more than it would be on strong versions of the biological outlook often found in evolutionary psychology).

It is, however, possible to integrate biological perspectives on the emotions with either weak or moderate versions of constructivism. Volney Gay has examined the possible strategies for combining the sciences and humanities and observes that "adherents of the weak

version of constructivism tend to be moderate supporters of evolutionary psychology. They hold that cultures constrain emotionality but that each is the expression of core or universal emotions."[22] Adherents of weak constructivism contend that emotionality varies between people and cultures, but they concede that such differences are but variations on an underlying and unvarying biochemical reality. Émile Durkheim, Max Weber, Sigmund Freud, Claude Levi-Strauss, and Talcott Parsons are all examples of scholars who have held this view. All maintained that humans share certain biological commonalities, although cultures regulate both the manner in which and degree to which these biological tendencies are expressed. Adherents of the moderate version of constructivism go even further and suggest that "we are more than our genes, more than our inherited constraints; there is something sui generis and potentially free within human capacities."[23] This position argues for the social creation of many emotions that are often mistakenly considered biologically based.

Both weak and moderate versions of constructivism (which are the counterparts of moderate and weak biological outlooks) provide possibilities for genuine interdisciplinary exchange. Such exchange, we might note, makes possible a more nuanced understanding of the subtlety of emotions. And while the bulk of current opinion in emotion research currently supports bringing a weak version of constructivism to an interpretation of wonder, we are far from arriving at closure on these important theoretical issues.

Debate also continues about the precise number of emotions found in humans. This debate is further complicated by a distinction between which emotions can be considered *primary* and which are *secondary*. Primary emotions are considered to be genetically based and, in general, controlled primarily by subcortical regions of the brain. Secondary emotions, on the other hand, are considered to be combinations or permutations of the primary emotions. Secondary emotions are also thought to be more influenced by social forces and individual experience. And, in contrast to primary emotions, secondary emotions are thought to be more connected with cortical

regions of the brain and for this reason to be more susceptible to conscious thought and control. Wonder would seem to fall more readily into the category of a secondary emotion. Wonder belongs to a family of emotions (i.e., surprise, curiosity, interest, joy) that seem to have a genetic basis. But a distinguishing characteristic of wonder is that it is connected with certain "higher-order" cognitive activities that suggest that it is more susceptible to cultural influence than those emotions almost wholly controlled by subcortical regions of the brain. Final closure on this point is not yet possible, but the balance of evidence would suggest that wonder is more amenable to personal and cultural variation than are those emotions typically categorized as primary.

We have already noted that between the third and eleventh centuries, Hindu philosophers enumerated nine basic emotions: sexual passion, amusement, sorrow, anger, fear, perseverance, disgust, serenity, and wonder.[24] The seventeenth-century philosopher René Descartes postulated six primary emotions (love, hatred, desire, joy, sadness, and wonder), with all other emotions being derived from this basic core.[25] Darwin, meanwhile, never enumerated any specific list of human emotions. Nor did he explicitly differentiate between which emotions are primary and which are secondary variations. Darwin did, however, devote specific chapters of *The Expression of the Emotions* to seven clusters of emotions that he believed could be detected in both animals and humans: (1) low spirits, anxiety, grief, dejection, despair; (2) high spirits, joy, love, tender feelings, devotion; (3) reflection, meditation, ill temper, sulkiness, determination; (4) hatred and anger; (5) disdain, contempt, disgust, guilt, pride, helplessness, patience; (6) surprise, astonishment, fear, horror; and (7) self-attention, shame, shyness, and modesty. It is not completely clear whether Darwin considered these clusters to be the primary emotions or whether they were just the ones he deemed most important for scientific study.

Since Darwin, scientific researchers have varied considerably in their categorization of primary emotions. Robert Plutchik has summarized the findings of selected researchers:[26]

THEORIST	PRIMARY EMOTIONS
Plutchik	fear, anger, sadness, joy, acceptance, anticipation, surprise
Scott	fear, anger, loneliness, pleasure, love, anxiety, curiosity
Tomkins	fear, anger, enjoyment, interest, disgust, surprise, shame, contempt, distress
Izard	fear, anger, enjoyment, interest, disgust, surprise, shame, contempt, distress, guilt
Ekman	fear, anger, sadness, happiness, disgust, surprise
Etude	fear, anger, sadness, joy, interest, surprise, distress, shame, shyness, disgust, guilt

Plutchik notes that virtually all recent theoretical models recognize fear, anger, and sadness as primary emotions. He adds that there is near consensus concerning joy, love, and surprise. Plutchik personally finds sufficient evidence to include disgust and anticipation on his list of primary emotions and then goes on to add such secondary or acquired emotions as ecstasy, adoration, amazement, pensiveness, distraction, and grief.

A word of caution needs to be interjected into any discussion of primary and secondary emotions. What Ben-Ze'ev calls the "subtlety of emotions" suggests that the feeling states to which we are referring (as well as their nature, causes, and consequences) are far too variable and complex to be neatly categorized. The best we can hope to do is to create plausible generalizations. The very concept of emotions is itself what Ben-Ze'ev calls a "prototypical category."[27] He goes on to suggest that various feeling states are to be considered emotions to the degree of similarity to the most typical case. The same applies to the argument for distinct emotion. The existence of distinct emotions is not an all-or-nothing affair; it is, rather, a matter of the degree of similarity to the most typical case. The point here is that we should resist premature foreclosure on any one definition of emotion in general, let alone distinct emotions. Indeed, "feeling states" are so elusive that in order to categorize them definitively we need far

greater understanding of the neural, cognitive, and phenomenological patterning of emotional experiences. The relatively primitive nature of our knowledge about emotions need not prevent us, however,
from proceeding cautiously and arriving at provisional understandings based on the overall fit between feeling states and prototypical
categories.

The fact that neither Plutchik nor any other Western scholar (at
least since Descartes in the seventeenth century) has listed wonder as
a primary emotion probably tells us much less about wonder than
about the philosophical assumptions underlying evolutionary-
adaptive theories. Plutchik, for example, begins his overview of emotions by highlighting a quotation on the frontispiece stating that
"science starts with fascination and wonder." Yet when identifying
distinct emotions he reveals an implicit tendency to focus attention
on what might be called "emotions of avoidance" rather than "emotions of enhanced rapport." Furthermore, Plutchik and most other
contemporary scientists tend to dwell on emotional experiences that
(1) manifest themselves over a short duration of time, (2) give rise to
visible facial expressions or bodily gestures, and (3) orient people to
concrete features of their physical environment. None of this bodes
well for the study of wonder as an emotional experience.

Although recent researchers have largely ignored the emotion of
wonder, some have investigated the evolutionary-adaptive functions
of other emotions with which wonder is closely associated. Jonathan
Haidt, for example, proposes a separate category of "moral emotions" that are linked to the interests or welfare of the social group to
which a person belongs.[28] Haidt argues that some emotions serve the
interests of the social group and therefore were "selected for" by
natural selection even though they do not appear to be favoring
short-term interests of individual members of the group. He points
out that there is extensive scientific evidence showing that emotions
such as disgust, contempt, shame, embarrassment, and guilt promote the long-term interests of a social group by inducing individuals to conform and contribute to group welfare. Haidt contends
that scientific researchers have inexplicably ignored the similar func-

tions served by the emotions of gratitude, awe, and wonder. He observes that "even less empirical research has been done on awe than gratitude—only 11 articles in PsycInfo have awe in the title or key phrase. . . . Frijda (1986) discusses *wonder* rather than awe, which he links to surprise and amazement and interprets as a passive, receptive mode of attention in the presence of something unexpected."[29]

Haidt is intrigued by Frijda's observation that wonder mobilizes physiological, perceptual, and cognitive changes that "enlarge the field of peripheral vision" and open our attention to a wider field of stimuli than we would ordinarily attend to.[30] Haidt further notes that wonder appears to be elicited by exposure to certain kinds of beauty and perfection. And, more important, wonder differs from other "moral emotions" such as disgust or embarrassment in that, rather than mobilizing defensive maneuvers, it "opens our hearts and minds" to other individuals in our social group: "[Awe and wonder] make people stop, admire, and open their hearts and minds. It may be for this reason that awe is so often discussed in a religious context as the proper and desirable response to the presence of God."[31]

Richard and Bernice Lazarus acknowledged the difficulty of categorizing wonder as an emotion in their *Passion and Reason: Making Sense of Our Emotions*. In a general discussion of aesthetic experiences that arouse a distinct class of emotions, they noted that sights of natural beauty often cause people to "feel awe or wonder, which can be likened to religious experience."[32] They had to confess, however, that to this point in their discussion of emotions they had "not treated mental states like awe and wonder as emotions, because these terms have more than one meaning and, quite frankly, we are not quite sure how to deal with them."[33] Wonder, they acknowledge, is a feeling state that "certainly seems to be emotional." They note that wonder is an "emotional reaction"—usually in response to discoveries about the world, its vastness, or the remarkable gifts of life and intelligence. They further conjecture that wonder may be blends of other emotions and observe that it has spiritual connotations because of the sense of mystery and tendency to produce both trust and

a sense of belonging. Conceding that wonder is different from most of the emotions usually described in social scientific literature, they conclude that it is "an emotional reaction that remains at the frontier of our understanding of the mind."[34]

Lazarus and Lazarus are surely correct that experiences of wonder remain at the frontier of our contemporary academic understanding of emotional reactions. Wonder is a complex and subtle emotional feeling. Yet despite this complexity and subtlety we can make some plausible generalizations. And while there may be no single essence that is a necessary and sufficient condition for all instances of wonder, there are prototypical characteristics of certain human experiences that make it meaningful to speak of wonder as a distinct emotional response.

A full account of the "prototypical characteristics" of wonder will be developed in the rest of this chapter and in subsequent ones. At the outset it must be stressed that wonder is first and foremost an experience. All human experience is shaped by the neural structure of our brains as well as our personal histories of interaction with our social and cultural environments. For this reason it is probably more helpful to think of wonder as an emotional experience (i.e., an activity whereby an organism responds to its environment) rather than as simply an emotion (i.e., a noun or separate entity somehow isolated from the multiple contexts in which it emerges). To repeat, wonder is not so much a separate "thing" as the feeling state accompanying the body's response to certain environmental situations. A preliminary definition of wonder, then, is that it is the feeling state that accompanies the total organism's response to something novel and unexpected (especially those things that strike us as especially powerful, real, true, and/or beautiful). The prototypical characteristics of this response can be assessed at any number of levels: the evolutionary-adaptive level, the neurophysiological level, the motivational level, the cognitive level, the attitudinal level, and—perhaps most important—the phenomenological level. No one level of analysis alone can tell us the whole story of the emotion of wonder.

Yet taken together, the various levels tell us much about the experience of wonder and about what typically characterizes a life shaped by wonder.

Motivational Functions of Distinct Emotions

Writing on the complex processes that collectively define our emotional life, Joseph LeDoux explains that emotions must be understood as "biological functions of the nervous system." Emotions, he further elaborated, are now known to be biologically based and shaped by evolution to perform specific adaptive tasks. He cautioned, however, that there is no one overall emotional center in the brain. Rather, "the various classes of emotions are mediated by separate neural systems that have evolved for different reasons." And, "if we are interested in understanding the various phenomena that we use the term 'emotion' to refer to, we have to focus on specific classes of emotions."[35] In other words, if we want to understand the emotion of wonder, we need to move beyond considering emotion as a general category and pursue the specific functions performed by the class of emotions to which wonder belongs.

Darwin did not include wonder among the emotions he enumerated in *The Expression of the Emotions in Man and Animals*. He did, however, consider the emotions of surprise and astonishment. He noted that "attention, if sudden and close, graduates into surprise; and this into astonishment; and this into stupefied amazement."[36] It is doubtful that he was equating wonder with "stupefied amazement" in that he described the latter as a frame of mind closely akin to terror. Yet he did note that there are distinct instances when surprise or astonishment leads to sustained amazement rather than to immediate action:

There is still another and highly effective cause, leading to the mouth being opened, *when we are astonished*, and more especially when we are suddenly startled. . . . Now when we start at any sudden sound or sight, almost all the muscles of the body are

involuntarily and momentarily thrown into strong action, for the sake of guarding ourselves against or jumping away from the danger, which we habitually associate with anything unexpected. But we always unconsciously prepare ourselves for any great exertion, as formerly explained, by first taking a deep and full inspiration, and we consequently open our mouths. *If no exertion follows, and we still remain astonished,* we cease for a time to breathe, or breathe as quickly as possible, in order that every sound may be distinctly heard. Or again, *if our attention continues long and earnestly absorbed,* all our muscles become relaxed, and the jaw, which was at first suddenly opened, remains dropped. Thus several causes concur toward this same movement, whenever *surprise, astonishment or amazement* is felt.[37]

Darwin analyzed astonishment and amazement in the context of what might be called "emotions of avoidance or defensiveness." He explains only their role in preparing organisms to respond to sudden sights and sounds. Their function is to ensure that we run or jump away from danger. Darwin does, however, seem to appreciate the possibility that some emotional responses may not give rise to immediate action. As he put it, if no exertion follows, then our attention continues long and earnestly absorbed. Unfortunately, Darwin failed to expand on how such "long and earnestly absorbed" attention might lead to very different kinds of adaptive behaviors. And for this reason Darwin failed to make any important contribution to our understanding of such emotions as interest, amazement, astonishment.

A more recent theorist, Sylvan Tomkins, is among those who view interest as a primary emotion. Tomkins maintained that the basic emotions are not a series of single emotional states but are instead parts of emotional families. He proposed, for example, that the basic emotion of anger is part of the emotional family that includes irritation, annoyance, assertion, and fury. Tomkins found that interest is part of the emotional family that includes curiosity, enthusiasm, and attraction.[38] Tomkins's association of interest with enthusiasm and

attraction helped him identify how this family of emotions motivates distinct kinds of adaptive behaviors. To the extent that interest and enthusiasm are paired, they will motivate sustained involvement with one's surroundings. Emotions such as interest, enthusiasm, and attraction thus mobilize behaviors very different from jumping, hiding, or running. Indeed, interest can sustain long-term constructive and creative interaction with the environment—thereby leading to distinctively human modes of biological and cultural adaptation.

One of Tomkins's collaborators, Carroll Izard, extended this perspective into a well-developed theory of how specific emotions perform distinct adaptive functions. One of the specific emotions that Izard studied is joy. Most studies of the evolutionary-adaptive functions of joy emphasize its role in creating situations likely to promote sexual contact. Izard, however, observes that joy performs other adaptive functions as well. For example, joy prompts smiles that serve as universally recognizable signals of readiness for friendly interaction. Joy, by the principles of contagion, empathy, and facial feedback, thus contributes to the well-being of the social group.

An even more important function performed by the emotion of joy is that it motivates us to engage life more fully and openly. "Joy heightens an openness to experience," noted Izard.

> Such openness in social situations can *contribute to affiliative behavior and the strengthening of social bonds.* Social bonds and the social support they provide create a highly adaptive mechanism that can easily be conceived as an advantage in evolution and development. In species in which the young experience a long period of dependency, a strong social bond between parent and offspring is essential to survival. No other emotion serves this function so effectively, providing significant benefits at little or no cost.[39]

Izard, like Tomkins, has also devoted considerable attention to the emotion of interest. Izard explains that the definition of the emotion of "interest" overlaps with the definitions of the terms "curiosity," "wonder," and "urge to explore or discover." His research suggests

that healthy people in a safe and comfortable environment experience interest more than any other emotion. The fact that interest spontaneously predominates consciousness in situations in which humans are free from immediate physical threat signals its significance for uniquely human modes of adaptation. According to Izard, "interest motivates exploration and learning, and guarantees the person's engagement in the environment. Survival and adaptation require such engagement. Interest supports creativity because it immerses one in the object or task and cues a sense of possibility. To paraphrase Tomkins, interest is the only emotion that can sustain long-term constructive or creative endeavors."[40]

Interest animates and enlivens the mind. It not only focuses attention on an object but also mobilizes us for engagement and interaction. For this reason the emotion of interest provides the motivation for constructive and creative endeavor, the development of intelligence, and personal growth.

Izard observes that interest most typically occurs in a pattern with joy. This connection can be seen, for example, in children's play, in which interest and joy combine in such a way as to sustain active engagement with the game. It appears as though the brain triggers joy as an internally generated reward for sustained interest in the surrounding world. Our brains seem to have evolved in ways that reinforce the development of intelligence and creative engagement with the environment.

This recognition of the interaction between interest and joy is a fruitful beginning point for a more thorough understanding of the emotion of wonder. As Izard pointed out, wonder is quite similar to the emotions of interest and joy. Wonder is the normal emotional response to unexpected stimuli or particularly vivid instances of vitality. It is true that wonder has no direct affect on the survival-oriented behaviors highlighted in most evolutionary accounts of the emotions. This is not, however, to say that wonder is irrelevant to humanity's adaptive strengths. Wonder, even more than interest, is a principal motivational source of what Tomkins and Izard describe as "long-term constructive or creative endeavors." Wonder is part of the

organism's strategic capacity to imbue the world with an alluring quality. Affectively, it leads to increased openness and receptivity rather than utilitarian action. Cognitively, it promotes contemplation of how the parts of life fit into some larger whole rather than analysis of how they can be broken down into still smaller (and ostensibly more manipulable) parts. To this extent wonder functions in ways that express uniquely human potentials for growth and intelligence.

The Neurophysiology of Wonder

To survive and produce viable offspring, all organisms must fend off predators, find food, and procreate. Organisms must, furthermore, take in and metabolize food sources. They must distinguish between prey and predator. And those that live in social units must be capable of minimizing intragroup discord, communicating intentions, and cooperating toward common goals. Natural selection favored anatomical structures conducive to these basic biological tasks. Among these anatomical structures are specific centers within the brain that regulate emotions (and therefore our motivation to think and behave in certain ways).

We are as yet a long way from a precise mapping of the brain structures governing specific emotions. Nonetheless, in recent years an extensive literature has emerged that has helped identify the basic neurophysiology of our emotional systems.[41] We might begin a summary of this literature by reminding ourselves that humans belong to the phylum Chordata, animals with backbones. The brain stem, located at the top of the spinal cord, contains the majority of neurological structures associated with essential physiological activities (e.g., digestion, respiration, simple locomotion). Compactly located within this region of the "primitive brain" are the pons (associated with salivation and chewing as well as the production of rapid eye movements during sleep), the medulla (coordinates respiration, heart rate, balance, facial movement), and the cerebellum (maintains

balance, receives auditory and visual information, coordinates motor movement).

Just above these brain structures and reaching into the midbrain are the thalamus and the limbic system. The thalamus receives input from the sensory organs and relays this information to other centers of the brain. The thalamus is sometimes referred to as the "gateway to the neocortex" because of its role as an intermediary between sensory organs and the more complex brain structures that determine behavioral strategies. The thalamus is, moreover, thought to regulate the specific emotions of panic or separation.

The limbic system is a group of subcortical structures that include the hypothalamus, the hippocampus, and the amygdala. This system is considered the principal center for regulating emotion and motivation. It does this in part by mediating and directing sensory input (of particular importance is the role of the limbic system in directing neural impulses to the cerebral cortex, where they are labeled, categorized, and interpreted prior to the determination of behavioral response). The part of the limbic system that has received the most attention is the amygdala, which has been consistently implicated in the production and regulation of emotions. It is important to note that neurophysiology is too complex to have as yet generated unambiguous evidence linking the amygdala to specific emotional processes.[42] It is clear, however, that the amygdala has neural connections with many other parts of the brain. It is also widely assumed that the amygdala plays an important role in assigning "emotional significance" to sensory input as it directs this input to appropriate regions of the brain. Of special importance is the possibility that the amygdala administers rewarding brain stimulation. This self-reinforcing stimulation increases the likelihood that individuals will engage in cognitive activities that enhance their overall well-being (such as Izard and Ackerman think is the case with wonder insofar as it seems to represent a combination of interest and joy).

The psychologist of religion Kelly Bulkeley points out that human emotion can never be fully explained in terms of the neural struc-

tures in the brain stem.[43] What distinguishes human cognition from that of other animals is the high ratio of cerebral cortex to brain stem and midbrain structures. The cerebral cortex contains between 9 billion and 12 billion neurons responsible for what we call the "higher intellectual" functions. Perhaps the most important region within the cerebral cortex is the "association cortex," which receives and processes sensory information. It is this processing activity within the association cortex that allows humans to behave in ways that are not completely determined by genetic and environmental influences. As one neurological textbook describes, the association cortex is devoted to "higher-order integrative functions that are neither purely sensory nor purely motor, but associative . . . [that serve] to associate sensory inputs to motor response and perform those mental processes that intervene between sensory inputs and motor outputs."[44] The great number of ways in which the association cortex can potentially combine sensory input into programs for behavioral action is what makes humans appear free and capable of self-determination.

The cerebral cortex is what enables humans to be cultural organisms. Cognitive development in humans is only partly hardwired by our genetically encoded programs. Experience, learning, and cultural patterns become part of our memories stored in the cerebral cortex and, in turn, influence the way that sensory input is labeled, categorized, and translated into behavioral strategies. Emotions in all likelihood have neurophysiological foundations that are innate and genetically governed. But in humans these genetic patterns invariably interact with the cognitive patterns shaped by experience and culture.

We are, to be sure, far from understanding the neurophysiology of emotions with anything close to certainty. But it seems prudent to acknowledge that all specific emotions, including the emotion of wonder, almost certainly involve an activation of neural activities in the limbic system and the centers of association in the cerebral cortex. All strong physiological reactions to environmental stimuli would entail the selective activation of the limbic system and hypothalamus. It would seem, however, that a distinguishing character-

istic of wonder is that it simultaneously involves the activation of the association cortex (as mediated through the amygdala). Humans differ from other mammals in the relatively greater size and activity of the association cortex, whose purpose is to "intervene between sensory inputs and motor outputs." Experiences of wonder are triggered by encounters with novel and unexpected stimuli. Wonder thus accompanies sensory input that defies existing associative categories and exceeds current boundaries of understanding. Kelly Bulkeley concludes that it is thus likely that "experiences of wonder have widespread and powerfully stimulating effects on the association cortex, expanding the functional range of those 'intervening' mental processes. . . . They compel the creation of new, more expansive categories and new, more subtly integrated modes of understanding."[45]

What distinguishes the experience of wonder from most other emotional experiences is that even though it occurs while the association cortex is active, it does not usher in immediate, goal-oriented behavior. Wonder, instead, is associated with a recognition and contemplation of the intrinsic significance of the stimuli at hand. As Bulkeley observes, wonder is typically characterized by a strong sense of the fullness of the present, which has the effect of "dethroning ordinary plans, purposes, and motivations. Many experiences of wonder are characterized by an unusual receptivity and radical openness."[46]

This last feature of wonder—the temporary deactivation of our utilitarian striving and the creation of a sense of our participation in a more general order of life—is crucial to understanding how wonder guides our adaptation to the wider interpersonal, moral, and cultural environments we inhabit.

3. A Life Shaped by Wonder: John Muir

I think that one of the properties of that compound
which we call humanity is that when exposed to the rays
of mountain beauty it glows with joy.—JOHN MUIR

THE PREVIOUS CHAPTER SHED LIGHT ON SOME OF THE
biological underpinnings of the experience of wonder. We
might pause here and become more attentive to the subtlety
of emotions in a single life. Any attempt to understand the prototypical characteristics of wonder must pay attention to the intercon-
nection of three levels of explicating human experience: biology (i.e.,
neurophysiology and evolutionary-adaptive functions); psychology
(i.e., distinctive modes of perception, cognition, motivation, and
interpersonal relationships); and phenomenology (i.e., the full, lived
range of thought and feeling as registered by the experiencing subject). It is the last of these that is most likely to yield insight into the
subtle links between emotional states, moods, attitudes, and philosophical sensibilities. An emotional experience is ordinarily thought
of as a feeling state that lasts a few seconds or, at most, a few minutes.
Yet emotional tendencies can also affect motivation, perception, and
cognition in ways that exert identifiable influences lasting days or
weeks (moods) and even years (personality traits).[1] These influences,

in turn, predispose individuals to certain philosophical and spiritual orientations to their world.

A philosopher by the name of Juan De Pascuale recently reflected on how experiences of wonder can have a profound effect on a person's existential posture toward life. He wrote that, more than any one other trait, it "is our capacity for wonder at the mystery of being that makes us human and separates us from the rest of creation."[2] Wonder, as no other emotion, prompts us to ask, "Why is there anything at all and not, rather, nothing?" The very act of asking this question acknowledges a deepened sense of our relationship to the universe. De Pascuale observes, "Prior to the experience of wonder, I now realize, I took the full weight of existence for granted as most people do most of the time." Wonder sets everyday existence against the context of the ultimate cause without which there would be no life. It therefore prompts existential response, not just to specific life circumstances but also to this "ultimate" context. De Pascuale explains that "the experience of wonder brings the world into relief and makes a person take life seriously. In wonder you realize that this is it. You have the opportunity to swim through the river of life rather than just float on it, to *own* your life rather than be *owned* by it."[3]

De Pascuale acknowledges that many people live out their lives without giving much thought to the mystery of existence. His point is that such people are far more likely to drift through life with little sense of their role in the larger cosmic drama. The experience of wonder disrupts the everyday routines of work and provides a chance to become more aware of just what and where we are. "If attended to, the experience of wonder gives birth to self-examination and to a mindful awareness of the world. In time you come to know yourself as you have been and are—and this gives you the possibility of choosing *how* to be. Through the experience of wonder we become true individuals and true citizens of the universe."[4]

History provides us with many examples of people whose experiences of wonder proved to be powerful catalysts for self-examination. Some individuals, it seems, stand apart as exemplars of wonder. Their lives demonstrate in particularly dramatic fashion how the emotion

of wonder gives rise to a "mindful awareness" of ourselves and our world. Their experiences of wonder set them on a course to becoming "true individuals and true citizens of the universe." Three such exemplars of wonder readily come to mind. John Muir, William James, and Rachel Carson all exhibited lives profoundly shaped by the emotion of wonder. There are, of course, numerous other people whose lives illustrate the way in which wonder opens up "the possibility of choosing how to be." The selection of these, and only these, exemplars of wonder is admittedly arbitrary. Nonetheless, these three provide fascinating case studies of the role that a particular kind of emotional experience might play in motivating distinctive perceptual, cognitive, and moral orientations to life. And, for this reason, their lives furnish important clues about how the experience of wonder shapes us in ways that we might become true citizens of the universe.

Immersion in Godful Beauty

Born in Dunbar, Scotland, John Muir (1838–1914) would eventually become the earliest leader of the American nature preservation movement. Muir served as the founding president of the Sierra Club and was the principal instigator of the National Parks System, which became the model for such systems worldwide.[5] All of this was rather unlikely for the Scottish boy raised in a stern Protestant family that subscribed to the view that God commanded humans to have complete dominion over the earth. John's father, Daniel Muir, believed the Bible to be God's inerrant revelation to humanity and therefore the only book that human beings can possibly require in their journey toward heaven. Daniel saw to it that his oldest son memorize God's holy commandments. John later recalled, "Father made me learn so many Bible verses every day that by the time I was eleven years of age I had about three fourths of the Old Testament and all of the New by heart and by sore flesh. I could recite the New Testament from the beginning of Matthew to the end of Revelation without a single stop."[6]

Apparently the constant threat of corporal punishment motivated John to commit the Bible to memory, but not to his heart. He found his greatest boyhood happiness away from home while playing with friends or even strolling alone in the nearby fields and woods. He recalled, "I loved to wander in the fields to hear the birds sing, and along the seashore to gaze and *wonder* at the shells and seaweeds, eels and crabs in the ponds among the rocks."[7] John's exploration of the surrounding countryside was abruptly halted when his father decided to uproot his family and immigrate to the United States. Economic conditions were harsh in Scotland. Yet Daniel Muir's desire to relocate to the New World was motivated by more than the quest for economic opportunity. He had just joined the fledgling Protestant sect known as the Disciples of Christ. Its members believed that their Bible-centered faith was restoring the simple ways of the primitive Christian church. Converts to this evangelical sect realized the godly opportunity provided by America's western frontier. Here, in a land not yet corrupted by errant forms of Christianity, this newly gathered community of believers might at last establish Christ's kingdom on earth.

After a forty-seven-day journey across the Atlantic, the Muir family arrived in the New World, eventually purchasing farmland near Kingston, Wisconsin. For the next ten years John worked more than sixty hours a week breaking sod, plowing fields, bringing in harvests, and repairing equipment. It was hard, solitary work—often performed while his father stayed indoors studying the Bible or traveling to neighbors' homes to preach the gospel. Yet in many ways John welcomed his harsh life because it kept him outdoors and surrounded by pristine nature. John was energized by his entrance into the "wonderful schoolless, bookless American wilderness." In Wisconsin he found "no more grammar, but boundless woods full of mysterious good things."[8] Life in rural Wisconsin fated John to meeting very few people during his adolescence. Yet he was constantly surrounded by wildlife that excited his capacity for wonder, thereby instilling a distinctive cognitive and perceptual orientation to the world. Years later

he recounted, "This sudden plash into wilderness—baptism in Nature's warm heart—how utterly happy it made us! Nature streaming into us, wooingly teaching her *wonderful* glowing lessons."[9]

Immersion in nature directed John's attention to unexpected phenomena. He remembers, for example, how he "used to wonder how the woodpeckers could bore holes so perfectly round, true mathematical circles." The odd path blazed by forest fires would set him "wondering why all the trees and everybody and everything did not share the same fate." Or, while watching mosquitoes select their targets, he was prompted to "wonder more and more at the extent of their knowledge."[10] Thus from an early age John was constitutionally susceptible to the emotion of wonder. He responded to unexpected perceptions of beauty, order, or vitality by setting these phenomena in ever larger contexts. This sense of "something more" that mysteriously manifested itself in Wisconsin's flora and fauna was for him nothing less than a continuing stream of divine epiphanies. He was "urged on and on through endless, inspiring, Godful beauty."[11]

As John neared the age of twenty, it became increasingly difficult for him to concede to his father's stern authoritarianism. One manifestation of his rebelliousness was a newfound interest in reading Shakespeare, Milton, and virtually every other nonbiblical text he could put his hands on. A second avenue for exerting his independence was his penchant for tinkering with mechanical devices. Both struck his father as careless diversions from responsible work and obedience to God's only true revelation. But John persevered. In time he invented several new mechanical devices such as clocks, thermometers, and a contraption that could arouse someone from sleep in the morning by jolting him or her out of bed. Finally, at the age of twenty-two and despite his father's objections, John gathered up his inventions and traveled to Madison so that he could display them at a state exposition. His inventions caught the attention of many of those who attended the exposition. A few encouraged him to develop his inventive prowess further and succeeded in talking John into enrolling in the University of Wisconsin.

While studying at the University of Wisconsin John was greatly

John Muir (Courtesy of the Library of Congress)

influenced by a Professor J. D. Butler, a Professor Ezra Carr, and—especially—Carr's wife, Jeanne. Both Professor Butler and Jeanne Carr introduced John to the writings of the romantic poets as well as the writings of the American Transcendentalists, such as those of Henry David Thoreau and Ralph Waldo Emerson (whom Jeanne Carr knew personally). These writings helped John build a bridge away from his father's narrow biblical religion to a wider world of thought and feeling. After a few years of taking classes (selected somewhat randomly rather than adhering to a fixed curriculum) and a brief sojourn through Canada to avoid the draft during the Civil War, John at last realized it was time to leave the University of Wisconsin for what he called "the university of the wilderness." Despite his aptitude for mechanical work, he feared spending any more of his time among machines. In his opinion the world of machines strives to reduce the living flow of nature to rule and order. He yearned instead for more sustained immersion in Godful beauty.

A brief sojourn through several southeastern states finally led to California's Sierra range. For the next seven years these mountains were John Muir's home—or more accurately, his temple, because it was in the mountains that he was fully baptized in the higher powers at work in the universe. And it was in the mountains that he was instructed in a moral vision that enables us to remain faithful to those higher powers.

Muir's time in the Sierras was a catechism conducted by the emotion of wonder. It started the moment he began letting go of his accustomed way of seeing things and allowed himself to be guided by the fresh perceptions available to him. His journals and letters are striking in this regard. They provide insight into the sequence of unexpected perspectives that jarred Muir out of older perceptual patterns and invited him to view life from new, higher-order conceptual frameworks. The grand vistas provided by mountain ranges and wide valleys provided perspectives that readily invited him to widen the scales he might use to measure and interpret the significance of an object or event. Muir's growing knowledge of geological time also enabled him to see life from unexpected perspectives. He might, for

example, focus his attention on a simple raindrop. But as he began to view this raindrop against the vast context of geological time, he unexpectedly found himself rapt with wonder: "How interesting to trace the history of a single raindrop! . . . since the first raindrop fell on the newborn leafless Sierra. . . . [Each drop is] God's messenger, angel of love sent on its way with majesty and pomp and display of power that make man's greatest shows ridiculous."[12]

Muir was aware that his experiences in the Sierras were significantly altering his perception and cognition. Against the vast vistas afforded by the mountains, he was no longer able to organize experience with accustomed notions of time, background/foreground, and causality. He once wrote his brother that "the forest trees seemed to be running round in a circle chase and all the streams by the roadside seemed to be running uphill."[13] One of his Muir's biographers, Michael Cohen, has observed that he was leaving the world of machines and entering a mystical perspective.[14] To Muir, nature now flowed in patterns that transcended scientific laws. When viewing mountain peaks at dawn, for example, Muir saw that they were "pervaded with the soul of light . . . they are made one, unseparate, unclothed, open to the Divine Soul, dissolved in the mysterious incomparable Spirit of holy Light."[15] The real way to apprehend nature, according to Muir, was in a perceptual mode filled with "rejoicing and wondering." Michael Cohen has aptly noted that "if a reader learned anything from [Muir's] narration, it was not what to see but how to see it. . . . He tried to make his readers powerful and enthusiastic observers, like himself. They would believe in the divine beauty."[16]

The Naturalist as Cultural Visionary

Muir likened the "rejoicing and wondering" engendered by natural beauty to the sacrament of baptism. It made all things new. The change in perceptual and cognitive styles "fertilized and stimulated and developed [the mind] like sun-fed plants."[17] Such rejuvenation, however, spontaneously ushers in a new understanding of the world.

As Stephen Fox has remarked, Muir's newly acquired sensibility made it possible for him to see "that the reductive tendency of modern science in breaking knowledge into ever smaller pieces of specialization obscured the whole picture."[18] Muir now saw unities, not fragments. His new sensibility took him beyond an anthropomorphic vision of nature. Having shifted to a perceptual frame of reference that wasn't circumscribed by the human ego, Muir acquired a truly biocentric vision of nature. He could see that humans are but one small part of a vaster whole. As he put it, the "freshness of perception" that the wilderness inspires in us helps us to "lose consciousness of our separate existence; you blend with the landscape and become part and parcel of Nature."[19] Muir could, moreover, see that this larger whole was not constructed for benevolence to humans. The wonder-driven changes in Muir's perceptual and cognitive orientation to the world drew him beyond an egocentric or even anthropocentric perspective of the world. He became, in other words, maximally aware of the intrinsic value of all forms of life and minimally aware of their relationship to human desires or aspirations. Wonder led him to see the value of nature wholly independent of human need or desire. He came to see that rattlesnakes, tarantulas, floods, and earthquakes deserve to be viewed as "realized ideas of God's mind" just as much as humans.

John Muir's close friend Jeanne Carr arranged for him to meet Ralph Waldo Emerson during the Transcendentalist philosopher's trip to California in 1871. While out for a walk together, Emerson made a telling remark to his newfound colleague: "The wonder is that we can see these trees and not wonder more!"[20] Emerson, like Muir, had been transformed by wonder-filled experiences in nature. Emerson, too, had been led to a new vision of life that avoided the narrowness often associated with both scientism and biblical religion. It was Emerson who in 1836 wrote that when he was alone in nature, "all mean egotism vanishes. I become a transparent eyeball; I am nothing; I see all; the currents of the Universal Being circulate through me; I am part and parcel of God."[21] Emerson's writings celebrated the potential that he believed every person has to open

him- or herself to a range of sensations ordinarily excluded by the waking rational mind. When we do finally open ourselves to receive an influx of this vaster universe, we experience "that shudder of awe and delight with which the individual soul always mingles with the Universal Soul."[22]

Muir had been acquainted with Emerson's thought for some time. Both Professor Butler and Jeanne Carr brought Emerson's writings to his attention while he studied at the University of Wisconsin. After their meeting in California, the two continued to exchange copies of their professional writing. When Muir now began reading Emerson's work more diligently, he found it falling short of the full wonder that trees are capable of inspiring. Emerson, for example, wrote that sometimes the woods and waters fail "to yield a present satisfaction. This disappointment is felt in every landscape." Muir scribbled his rejoinder in the margins of the text: "No—always we find more than we expect." In another spot Emerson suggested that "trees are imperfect men" because they are rooted in the ground, to which Muir responded with an emphatic "No." And when Emerson conjectured that squirrels and bees toil endlessly without knowing what they do, Muir countered, "How do we know this?" It would thus seem that Stephen Fox is correct in concluding that for all the influence that the writings of Emerson and Thoreau had on the development of Muir's thought, their influence was really that of corroborating the ideas that grew out of Muir's own mystical rapport with nature.[23]

Among those ideas that Emerson and Thoreau corroborated was Muir's growing pantheism. Muir frequently referred to nature as a temple, a manifestation of spiritual power. The wilderness was itself divine, teeming with the mysterious spirit of holy Light. This implied, of course, that those who fully open themselves to the wilderness thereby align themselves with the ultimate cause of life. Muir was himself a symbol of this ecstatic pantheism. He recounted, for example, an instance in which he found himself dangling from a steep cliff. His death seemed imminent. The danger set his mind reeling until, in a single moment, he reached a state of "preternatural clearness." Muir recounts that he "seemed suddenly to become pos-

sessed of a new sense. The *other self*, bygone experiences, instinct, or guardian angel,—call it what you will,—came forward and assumed control. Then my trembling muscles became firm again, every rift and flaw in the rock was seen as through a microscope, and my limbs moved with a positiveness and precision with which I seemed to have nothing at all to do."[24]

Much in the way that Emerson's "mean egotism" had to vanish to enable the currents of Universal Being to flow through him, Muir, too, found that certain unusual states of mind enable "the other self" to come forward and assume control. An even clearer instance occurred during his first summer in the Sierras when "suddenly, and without warning," he became convinced that his former mentor Professor Butler of the University of Wisconsin was below him in the valley. Although the idea was highly improbable, he couldn't let it go. The very next day he "found Professor Butler as the compass-needle finds the pole. So last evening's telepathy, transcendental revelation, or whatever else it may be called was true. . . . This seems the one well-defined marvel of my life of the kind called supernatural; for, absorbed in glad Nature, spirit-rappings, second sight, ghost stories, etc., have never interested me since boyhood, seeming comparatively useless and infinitely less wonderful than Nature's open, harmonious, songful, sunny, everyday beauty."[25]

Muir, then, was not prone to supernaturalism per se. Even this "well-defined marvel" struck him as "less wonderful" than nature's everyday beauty. As Catherine Albanese has noted, Muir's supernaturalism was a "muted" one in that he located spiritual power in the stuff of the earth rather than in some heaven beyond the stars.[26] His wilderness experiences made him sensitive to forces within nature that are different from those recognized by science or by our churches. His peculiar way of apprehending nature through "rejoicing and wondering" enabled him to see how this transcendent order of things constitutes a pattern or harmony not otherwise discernible. Thus, even though Muir embraced Darwin and was a thoroughgoing evolutionist, he was yet unwilling to reduce nature to purely mechanical forces. Where Darwin saw a world controlled purely by the inter-

play of chance and struggle, Muir perceived only the wholeness of nature and the "mystery of harmony." Muir's distinctive perceptual and cognitive orientation to experience enabled him to look past material and efficient causes and see the causal presence of a "higher" harmony: "Evolution!—a wonderful, mouth-filling word, isn't it! . . . Somewhere, before evolution was, was an Intelligence that laid out the plan, and evolution is the process, not the origin, of the harmony."[27]

Muir's wilderness experiences altered his perspective in ways that led him to see how nature functions as a unified organism. This vision carried with it a pantheistic sense of the sacredness of all being—putting Muir at the forefront of nineteenth- and early twentieth-century thought about the environment. This vision carried over into his efforts to establish the national parks movement and, with his founding of the Sierra Club, one of the most important conservationist societies in history. As the entry on Muir in *The Encyclopedia of Nature and Religion* concludes, "even when losing important battles, Muir's passionate writing contributed to shifts in public perceptions that help account for the continuing strength of preservationist sentiment in the United States. His thought has become nearly canonical within the contemporary environmental movement—and deep ecologists have posthumously adopted Muir as a central intellectual and spiritual elder—precisely for his 'resacralization' of nature—a perceptive task they view as a prerequisite to the re-establishment of proper human behavior toward the natural world."[28] It seems, then, that Muir's lasting contribution to the world was not just what to see in nature but how to see it. Muir taught us that learning to behold nature in a manner permeated by "rejoicing and wondering" is the important first step toward becoming a citizen of an ecologically healthy universe.

4. Adaptation and Humanity's Appetite for Wonder

We have an appetite for wonder. . . . It is my thesis that the
spirit of wonder . . . is the very same spirit that moves
great scientists . . . [and] might inspire still greater poetry.
—RICHARD DAWKINS, evolutionary biologist

JOHN MUIR'S LIFE WAS SHAPED BY RECURRING EXPERI-
ences of wonder. He responded to displays of natural beauty by
becoming relatively quiescent and by organizing his perceptions
in ways that led to a basically pantheistic view of the relatedness and sacredness of all being. It is not surprising that both the
natural and social sciences have shied away from the study of emotional experiences such as these. Wonder, after all, does not display
the "prototypical characteristics" associated with the evolutionary-
adaptive model underlying most contemporary discussions of the
emotions. Experiences of wonder do not, for example, ordinarily
lead to the kinds of facial and physiological expressions found in the
primary emotions studied by most researchers. Nor do they contribute to the survival tasks closely linked with hunting and gathering.
Indeed, the experience of wonder has relatively little adaptive significance for single individuals in the short run. Yet, as we have seen in
the case of John Muir, experiences of wonder may prompt individ-

uals over time to develop moods and attitudes that serve the adaptive needs of the wider community. They can also give rise to religiously charged philosophical orientations that might possibly serve the long-term survival of the human species. The study of wonder thus prompts reflection on the fairly narrow understandings of "useful" and "adaptive" that the sciences traditionally bring to their study of emotional experience. Seen in wider anthropological context, experiences of wonder evoke moods and attitudes that lead to what may well be humanity's highest levels of fulfillment and well-being.

The Mind as Adaptive Agent

Darwin's interest in the biological question concerning why humans display emotions launched the academic discipline of evolutionary psychology. He organized his study of how the mind works around the assumption that the natural environment poses survival problems that must be successfully resolved if the organism is to survive and to produce viable offspring. It follows that natural selection shaped the human mind to solve these problems and guide our adaptation to the environment. Darwin was consequently less interested in what emotions *are* than in what they *do*. Emotions, like all other mental states, are part of human nature because they perform functions essential to adaptation and survival. This was certainly the case in Darwin's account of the emotions of surprise, astonishment, and amazement (the closest he came to studying wonder). According to Darwin, astonishment or amazement occurs when we are suddenly startled: "Now when we start at any sudden sound or sight, almost all the muscles of the body are involuntarily and momentarily thrown into strong action, *for the sake of guarding ourselves against or jumping away from the danger.*"[1] From an evolutionary perspective, the mind exists for the sake of guiding adaptation.

Several years ago Steven Pinker, a psychologist at the Massachusetts Institute of Technology, wrote a book entitled *How the Mind Works*. From the standpoint of evolutionary science, he explained, "the mind is a naturally selected neural computer." Genes build the

mind to ensure their own survival. For Pinker, as for Darwin, a properly scientific account of the mind focuses on what the mind does rather than on what it is: "The mind is what the brain does. . . . The mind is organized into modules . . . their operation was shaped by natural selection to solve the problem of the hunting and gathering lives led by our ancestors."[2]

Natural selection progressively shaped our minds to solve problems that were life-and-death matters to our ancestors. We have thus inherited mental capacities that correspond to "the key features of encounters among objects and forces, and the features of other consequential themes of the human condition such as fighting, food, and health."[3] Pinker contends that the logical implication of this fact is that our minds were built solely for the purpose of understanding objects and events in the physical world. They were not designed to answer abstract questions. Pinker concludes that philosophy, moral theory, and religion are futile endeavors. Our minds lack the cognitive equipment to answer the questions they raise.

Pinker readily admits that the natural world evokes wonder and awe in us. He argues, however, that such wonder and awe are misdirected if they lead us to contemplate abstract issues such as the meaning of life. Pinker contends that it is futile to think about the whole of reality. All of our ideas, even the most complicated, are built out of simpler ones. To Pinker it follows that "the meaning of the whole is determined by the meaning of the parts and the meaning of the relations that connect them."[4]

Pinker is not simply asserting that it is easier for the mind to identify parts or the discrete relations between them. He is instead laying down the ontological dictum that the meaning of the whole is exhaustively explained in this way. Pinker consequently views religion and philosophy as nonadaptive by-products of evolution; they are misguided attempts to apply "mental tools to problems other than the problems they were designed to solve."[5] This is particularly true of religion insofar as it consists of "the common folly of believing in the palpably untrue."[6]

The evolutionary psychologist Scott Atran also examines the evo-

lutionary origins and functions of the human mind. Atran explains that from the standpoint of natural selection the brain's principal task can be described as that of "agency detection." Emotions such as surprise or wonder would thus be explained as one of the brain's inherited tendencies for "agency detection in the face of uncertainty." Atran contends that cognitive schemata "for recognizing and interpreting animate agents may be a crucial part of our evolutionary heritage, which primes us to anticipate intention in the unseen causes of uncertain situations that carry the risk of danger or the promise of opportunity, such as predators, protectors, and prey."[7] Atran, like Pinker, believes that religion represents the misapplication of our brain's adaptive powers. When confronted with confusing or ambiguous events, our brains seek out their "unseen causes." It is thus fully understandable why many humans mistakenly come to believe in supernatural agents such as gods, ghosts, or angels. Unexpected phenomena frequently prompt our brains to seek "agency" in religious rather than scientific ways. Unfortunately, religious beliefs perpetuate ignorance of the surrounding world. Religious beliefs are based on the erroneous attribution of causal influence to supernatural beings and are therefore incapable of guiding us toward productive relations with the physical environment over the long run.

The eminent biologist Richard Dawkins has also applied evolutionary principles to understand how the mind works. Dawkins, moreover, is specifically interested in the origins and function of what he calls humanity's "appetite for wonder." He accounts for wonder by noting that "it is as if the nervous system is turned at successive hierarchical levels to respond strongly to the unexpected, weakly or not at all to the expected."[8] Dawkins's point is thus that wonder originates as a response to unexpected stimuli. Its primary function is to intensify our cognitive response to the world. He wants to make it clear, however, that only science adequately translates wonder into effective engagement with the environment. "It is my thesis," he explains, "that the spirit of wonder which led Blake to Christian mysticism, Keats to Arcadian myth, and Yeats to Fenians and fairies, is the very same spirit that moves great scientists, a spirit

which, if fed back to poets in scientific guise, might inspire still greater poetry."[9]

Dawkins never explains what the value of poetry is, much less why we might desire still greater poetry. Instead, we are told that humans "have an appetite for wonder . . . which real science ought to be feeding (rather than being fed by religious superstitions)."[10] Thus, while Dawkins recognizes the central importance of humanity's "appetite for wonder" in guiding us to productive relationships with the world, he believes that wonder has no normative value for this unless it eventuates in scientific rationality.

Despite their narrow philosophical commitments, Dawkins, Pinker, and Atran lay the foundations for an evolutionary-adaptive analysis of wonder. They have drawn attention to the role that natural selection has played in shaping mental activities. They have alerted us to the fact that our brains respond to uncertainty by selectively organizing information in such a way as to facilitate adaptation and survival. And they have also reminded us that the brain's most pressing concern is that of discerning agency and intention, especially in situations that are otherwise ambiguous. The brain is wired to seek those sources of causal agency, purpose, or intentionality that vitally impinge on our lives and thus make it possible for us to establish productive relationships with the surrounding world.

Where Pinker, Atran, and Dawkins prove unhelpful is their peculiar insistence that the only proper domain of adaptation is the immediate physical environment. The complexity of humans' cerebral cortex makes our species unique. The high ratio of cerebral cortex to brain stem permits tremendous flexibility in an organism's interaction with the environment. For this reason culture (as opposed to strict biology) plays an unprecedented role in human adaptation. As Konrad Lorenz observed, humanity's "whole system of innate activities and reactions is phylogenetically so constructed, so 'calculated' by evolution as to need to be complemented by cultural tradition."[11] Our brains coevolved with our cultural experience and symbolic communication. Higher-order cognition made cultural life

possible even as cultural life in turn selected for brains capable of engaging in abstract, higher-order thought.

Adaptation for humans is mediated by culture and interpersonal relationships. The environment that humans adapt to is not "out there" in any immediate or physical sense. Humans adapt to an environment that is fluid rather than static, social rather than physical, abstract rather than solely physical, and striving toward future possibilities rather than composed only of present realities. Insofar as Pinker, Atran, and Dawkins failed to emphasize these elements of human adaptation, they were destined to misunderstand the full adaptive significance of humanity's appetite for wonder.

It is surely true that evolution constructed brains designed to solve problems of causality in the physical domain (the domain of parts). This should not, however, blind us to the fact that evolution also selected for the family of emotions (e.g, joy and interest) to which wonder belongs. Wonder is also part of our organism's efforts to detect agency, but it does so by seeking the intentionality of a greater whole. Experiences of wonder respond to uncertainty by alerting us to the possible presence of a more general level of existence that—at least potentially—has causal relevance to our pursuit of well-being. Wonder, then, motivates efforts to contemplate—and even adapt to—orders of life that are not "out there" in any straightforward way. Pinker, Atran, and Dawkins are thus correct to alert us to the fact that wonder-driven thinking veers from objective fact. They are even right to decry the superstitiousness of wonder-driven thinking if it leads to hypothetical ideas that are unequivocally contradicted by ongoing experience. Emotions and beliefs that demonstrably impede hunting and gathering activities are surely counterproductive. If the emotion of wonder mistakenly leads to delusions, then it has clearly become maladaptive. But to think that evolution did not also favor thinking that goes beyond sensory input is ideology, not science. Indeed, some of the highest intellectual accomplishments of which humans are capable require the construction of hypothetical "higher orders" of existence.

To summarize, wonder is closely allied with other emotional experiences that arise in the perception of something novel, unexpected, or inexplicable. It, too, sets us in search of causality, agency, intentionality, and purpose amid these unexpected features of our environment. Yet wonder differs from the emotions ordinarily studied by evolutionary theorists for two reasons. First, wonder is an emotion linked with approach and affiliation rather than avoidance. As Jonathan Haidt put it, wonder opens our hearts and minds. It motivates a quest for increased connection with the putative source of unexpected displays of life, beauty, or truth. This ordinarily requires increased openness or receptivity rather than instrumental action. Wonder is thus somewhat rare among the emotions in its functional capacity to motivate people to venture outward into increased rapport with the environment. Second, wonder awakens our mental capacity for abstract, higher-order thought. Indeed, it seems to direct our cognitive activities to construct models of a greater whole in terms of which the parts of our lives might be seen to have meaning and purpose. Far from making wonder a futile misdirection of our adaptive powers, these are precisely the traits that enable wonder to assist humanity in obtaining the highest kinds of satisfaction and fulfillment.

Wonder, Receptivity, and Adaptation

It is curious that Pinker, Atran, and Dawkins—like so many in the field of evolutionary psychology—focus almost exclusively on the role that natural selection plays in shaping the course of evolution. Darwin, after all, described evolution in terms of the interplay between two independent variables: natural selection and free variation (i.e., mutation). Free variation is the random process whereby organisms generate accidental changes or variations in their own structure. Such changes are produced spontaneously and are not caused by the surrounding environment. Free variations give organisms wholly new attributes that they bring to their interactions with the environment. True, it is the environment that selects for or against

these novel changes. But the initial source of evolutionary change exists in the spontaneous variations that individual organisms bring to experience (rather than being the result of environmental forces).

In humans this tendency toward free variation is almost exclusively cultural rather than biological. We introduce change into the environment through our ideas, thoughts, and beliefs. The human mind is not merely a passive organ. Its capacity to guide our adaptation to the world is not limited to conforming to the brute realities of the external environment. The human mind is an active agent. It brings its own, internally created agenda to experience. The mind actively shapes sensory input by labeling and categorizing it in ways that appear most suited to its own desires and interests. Important, too, is the fact that the human mind is not totally in the service of basic drives such as hunger, thirst, physical defense, and sexual reproduction. Humans in every culture have been motivated to satisfy any number of other, nonsurvival needs or interests: art, humor, play, morality, friendship, philosophy, and religion. Each of these emerged first in human evolution as a free variation that individuals brought to the environment. Mental activities that have little to do with the skills of hunting and gathering thus have played a tremendous role in the development of behaviors aimed at meeting a wide range of distinctly human satisfactions.

Creative adaptation is always a result of a delicate interplay between organism and environment.[12] Individual organisms change, influence, and select certain aspects of the environment even as the environment changes, influences, and selects certain aspects of the organism. Successful adaptation will, over the long run, entail two distinct but interconnected movements: (1) the movement whereby the organism adjusts itself to fit the environment and (2) the movement in which the environment in some way is shaped or mastered to fit the species.

Not only do these two movements adequately reflect adaptive processes at the biological level, but they also reflect adaptation over the course of our individual lives and of cultural institutions. For example, Jean Piaget, the noted specialist in cognitive development,

accounts for ongoing cognitive development as the interplay between assimilation and accommodation. David Bakan used slightly different terminology when he spoke of adaptation requiring agency and communion.[13] Agency here refers to adaptation through active mastery, while communion refers to adaptation through receptivity. Ernest Schactel spoke of optimal psychological growth requiring alternation between what he called the autocentric (i.e., oriented to manipulate the environment) and allocentric (i.e., motivated to become more open or receptive to the environment) modes of perception.[14] Arthur Deikman used the terms "activity" and "receptivity" to refer to the two psychological tasks of actively structuring experience in ways that serve utilitarian needs and envisioning the world in more holistic, spatial, and relational ways.[15] And, finally, the sociologist Max Weber used a similar distinction to categorize the adaptive functions performed by the world's religions. His distinction between mystical religion and moralistic or ascetic religion was predicated on his understanding of adaptation through adjustment (internal changes in the self) and adaptation through mastery (external organization of reality).[16]

Don Browning, a theologian and psychologist of religion, has carefully explained that creative adaptation necessitates both of these basic adaptive modalities.[17] The active mode of seeking environmental mastery is necessary for human survival. Humans must create a world in which to live. They cannot simply conform to the physical environment as it is. Active, willful mastery of the environment is required of us if we are to build and order a world.

The active mode, however, is not sufficient for creative adaptation to the environment. In fact, it becomes destructive if not continuously balanced by the receptive mode. Active mastery enables us to build and manipulate a world, but it can also foster a kind of tunnel vision that makes us blind to the realities (e.g., ecological, ethical, interpersonal) of the larger environment in which we live. This is where the more receptive mode becomes crucial to adaptation. We need to break out of our constructed world from time to time and gain a larger vision of the full range of our needs and interests. We

need to see ourselves as part of a larger whole. As Browning explains, the receptive mode helps us "get in touch with the unitary and relational aspects of reality. It gives us a vision of our relatedness to the world, to other human beings, and to God. To this extent, the receptive mode is responsible for our visions of peace and wholeness which mark the religious sensibility."[18]

Evolutionary theorist Richard Dawkins was therefore right on target when he heralded humanity's "appetite for wonder" as our species' most distinctive attribute. It is wonder that most clearly reflects our capacity for creative adaptation to the world. Wonder makes possible "a vision of our relatedness to the world." It generates visions of peace and wholeness. The emotional experience of wonder brings a sense of the fullness of the present moment, the existential now. It dethrones ordinary plans, purposes, and motivations and makes us receptive to our participation in a more general order of life. It is for this reason that wonder is—as Dawkins points out—so intimately associated with great science and great poetry. Wonder responds to novel or uncertain life situations by compelling the creation of new, more expansive categories of understanding. It is thus a prime catalyst of free or spontaneous variations. Wonder excites the human mind to conceive of new needs and interests that often have little to do with immediate biological survival. The experience of wonder, then, is a principal source of humanity's creative adaptation. It spurs us to break loose of preconstructed models of our world to pursue quite novel interests—among which might include the quest for intrinsic meaning, the realization of social justice, or the artistic creation of particularly vivid examples of truth, beauty, or vitality.

We are now in a position to appreciate how the life story of John Muir suggests that emotional experiences might guide adaptation in far more subtle ways than is customarily represented by most social scientists. Experiences of wonder shaped Muir's life in such a way that "rejoicing and wondering" became central to his moods, dispositions, and personality traits. It might even be argued that Muir's wonder-driven emotional sensibilities are the very reason he was so horribly ill-adapted to the middle-class society of his own day. He

was emotionally unfit to earn a living in a capitalist society. He wasn't even able to win many of the important ecological battles of the time. Yet, as one of his biographers has shown, his experiences of wonder shaped his life in ways that enabled him to exert a powerful influence over the long haul of history. Experiences of wonder shaped Muir's way of perceiving. They enabled him to see how natural landscapes are "open to the Divine Soul, dissolved in the mysterious incomparable Spirit of holy Light!" His life and writings have helped others learn to experience the same kind of wonder. And thus, even when Muir was losing important battles, his "passionate writing contributed to shifts in public perceptions that help account for the continuing strength of preservationist sentiment in the United States. His thought has become nearly canonical within the contemporary environmental movement—and deep ecologists have posthumously adopted Muir as a central intellectual and spiritual elder—precisely for his 'resacralization' of nature—a perceptive task they view as a prerequisite to the re-establishment of proper human behavior toward the natural world."[19] Experiences of wonder, by giving us a new vision of our relatedness to the world, can prove powerfully important to humanity's long-term biological and cultural fitness.

We might, then, expand on Dawkins's insight that it is our appetite for wonder that inspires both poetry and science. Our appetite for wonder is also what makes human evolution so open ended and truly creative.

Culture, Religion, and the Ritualization of Wonder

The human brain has been calculated by evolution to require extra-somatic sources of information. Instinct alone cannot shape behavior in ways that serve our long-term needs and interests. Our biology needs to be complemented by cultural tradition. Cultures therefore emerged to perform evolutionary-adaptive functions. The term "culture" here refers to systems of symbols and norms that define and guide a society and the individuals within it. These symbols

convey a society's goals or purposes and some of the preferred means or strategies for accomplishing these ends.

It was with this functional understanding of culture in mind that anthropologist Clifford Geertz defined religion as a "cultural system." Geertz's point is that religion provides many of the cultural patterns that shape both social and psychological reality. From an anthropological point of view, "religion is (1) a system of symbols which acts to (2) establish powerful, pervasive, and long-lasting *moods and motivations* in men by (3) formulating conceptions of a general order of existence and (4) clothing these conceptions with such an aura of factuality that (5) the moods and motivations seem uniquely realistic."[20] It is safe to assume that by "moods and motivations" Geertz was thus acknowledging the centrality of emotions in the human motivational system. And, more specifically, Geertz was associating religion with emotions that orient us to "a more general order of existence" in terms of which human behavior might be evaluated or judged. Geertz was, then, implicitly arguing that the emotion of wonder (and other closely allied emotions) is intimately connected with religion's ability to pattern human behavior according to cultural norms that are widely believed to have an objective reality and to be worthy of commanding our loyalty.

Religions—in order to perform their cultural function of patterning behavior—must establish links between our emotions and "conceptions of a general order of existence." By this Geertz and other social scientists mean that humans in all cultures quest for ultimate meanings and values. They seek to conform their lives to transcendent truths. Sociologist Peter Berger amplifies this point by explaining that "religion is the human enterprise by which a sacred cosmos is established."[21] Humans have a need to conform their lives to "the fundamental meanings inherent in the universe." Religion induces conformity to moral codes and other normative patterns "by bestowing upon them an ultimately valid ontological status, that is, by *locating* them within a sacred and cosmic frame of reference."[22]

From this anthropological perspective, the crucial part of religion

is "locating" human phenomena within a cosmic frame of reference. What distinguishes religion from other forms of cultural systems (e.g., political, economic, or scientific) is thus its particular mode of "seeing" or "apprehending" the world. Religion, as Geertz explains, fosters belief in conceptions of a general order of existence by inculcating a very particular emotional sensibility: "The religious perspective differs from the common-sensical in that . . . it moves *beyond the realities of everyday life to wider ones* which correct and complete them, and its defining concern is *not action upon those wider realities but acceptance* of them, faith in them."[23]

Religion differs from the scientific perspective in that it questions the realities of everyday life not out of methodological skepticism but out of an emotion-based sensibility for "a wider reality." If religion is to succeed in its cultural role, then, it must ritualize experiences that provide a felt sense of this wider reality. It seems reasonable to assume that the ritualization of experiences of wonder is one of the principal strategies by which religion has historically fostered "moods and motivations" thought to be connected with a wider reality. As we saw in the life and thought of John Muir, experiences of wonder prompt us to look beyond the immediate physical environment to a more general order of existence. Wonder, moreover, imbues the world with a certain "luring" quality—it invites us to seek enhanced rapport or harmony with, not utilitarian mastery of, this more general order of existence. Wonder leads to increased openness or receptivity rather than instrumental action. And, importantly, wonder awakens our mental capacity for abstract, higher-order thought. It sets us searching for the relationship of the particulars of our life with meanings or purposes intrinsic to this more general order of existence.

It seems, in fact, that almost every human culture possesses rituals specifically designed to induce emotional states that include elements of awe and wonder. In her book *Ecstasy, Ritual, and Alternate Reality*, anthropologist Felicitas Goodman observes that religious rituals often accomplish a kind of "brain tuning."[24] Religious rituals arouse emotions that enable us to believe that we are momentarily

"tuning" into another order of reality. Encounters with this alternate order of reality—whether mild or ecstatic—forever change a person's understanding of the nature and meaning of his or her life. Forces and powers whose existence had never before been suspected are thereafter believed to be crucial variables affecting the person's quests for wholeness and fulfillment.

It is quite possible that many religious rituals are effective precisely because of their ability to elicit neurophysiological reactions similar to those that accompany the experience of wonder. Andrew Newberg and Eugene d'Aquili used neural imaging technology to study the neurological activities associated with religious experience. They were primarily interested in studying quiescent experiences that people interpret as affording them a general sense of peace and "oneness" with a vaster spiritual reality. What they found was that such experiences were accompanied by a temporary deactivation of the "orientation association" region of the brain (i.e., the posterior section of the parietal lobe that processes sensory input needed to create a sense of the spatial location and boundaries of the body). As the orientation association region gradually slows down, the brain begins to construct altered perceptions of space, time, self, and ego in ways that produce new and mystical sensations. Newberg and d'Aquili found that religious experiences were accompanied by increased activity in the "attention association" area. They explain "that part of the reason the *attention association area* is activated during spiritual practices such as meditation is because it *is heavily involved in emotional responses*—and religious experiences are usually highly emotional. So it seems reasonable that the attention association area must have some important interaction with other brain structures underlying emotion during meditative and religious states."[25]

Newberg and d'Aquili thus suggest that religious states, like the experience of wonder, are characterized by the arousal of cognitive efforts to attend to novel stimuli combined with the seeming irrelevance of normal interpretive categories. Myth, because it communicates unusual notions of causality, resonates with the emotional system "when both the quiescent and arousal systems are simulta-

neously active."[26] They further observe that religious ritual is most effective when it alters our neurophysiology in such a way as to induce religious belief (particularly belief in the existence of something "more" than physical reality and the possibility of closing the distance between the self and this spiritual "more"). They argue that the mystical experiences of union produced by ritual acts are governed largely by the "biology of belief." Repetitive motor activity (e.g., ritualized dancing, drumming, chanting) in religious ceremonies can have significant effects on the amygdala and hypothalamus. Such ritual activities will, they conclude, almost inevitably be experienced as "religious awe."[27]

Awe and wonder are not the only emotions associated with religious myth and ritual. Shame, humility, fear, joy, and even anger or lust are among the many emotions that also accompany a culture's attempt to evoke a distinctively religious (rather than scientific or commonsensical) orientation to life. But awe and wonder are surely critical to religion's cultural task of inculcating distinctive moods and motivations. Recurring experiences of wonder provide an experiential template for belief in something "more" than ordinary reality. Ritual sights, smells, and actions arrest our attention and lure us into seeking deeper connection with that causal presence or power that somehow lies "beyond" the physical universe.

Religion, through the ritualization of wonder, sustains cultural paradigms that establish powerful, pervasive, and long-lasting moods and motivations. Moreover, wonder continually revitalizes such paradigms by connecting them with belief in a general order of existence, a cosmic frame of reference. It is thus not just our appetite for wonder but also our ability to ritualize wonder that fuels humanity's adaptive capacities.

5. A Life Shaped by Wonder: William James

Specifically religious experiences . . . soften nature's outlines and open out the strangest possibilities and perspectives.—WILLIAM JAMES

WE HAVE ALREADY NOTED JUAN DE PASCUALE'S OBSER-vation that "if attended to, the experience of wonder gives birth to self-examination and to a mindful awareness of the world."[1] No one better illustrates this transforma-tive experience than one of America's greatest philosophers and psychologists, William James. James stands out across history as an "exemplar of wonder" in part because several distinct experiences of wonder had a remarkable effect on his perceptual, cognitive, and moral orientations to life. More important, however, his mindful at-tention to these experiences furnished the experiential template for a full-blown philosophical outlook that is both spiritually and morally compelling even to this day.

The Experience of Metaphysical Illumination

William James (1842–1910) was born into a family that assured his early introduction to the major intellectual and religious debates that have

defined the modern era.[2] His father, Henry James Sr. had inherited a fortune that was large enough to permit him to devote all his energies to philosophical and theological investigations. Henry James Sr. was a close friend of the era's most progressive thinkers. Many of them, including Ralph Waldo Emerson, visited the James home frequently to engage in lively discussion. Henry became enamored of the era's innovative spiritual philosophies, particularly Swedenborgianism. Emanuel Swedenborg had been a preeminent European scientist before proclaiming that he had been visited by angelic beings who revealed to him the secrets of the universe. Swedenborg's metaphysical system hinged around the twin doctrines of correspondence (i.e., the belief that there are multiple levels or dimensions to the universe that are in essential harmony with one another) and influx (i.e., the belief that energies from a "higher" level of the universe can, under the precise lawful conditions, flow into a "lower" level and exert causal influences). Henry James extended Swedenborg's teachings in a series of largely ignored publications filled with grandiose metaphysical speculations.

Henry James was determined that his children would make original contributions to the world, and he provided them with expensive educations, private tutors, and numerous trips to European cultural centers. One son, Henry Jr., became a gifted novelist. But it was his oldest child, William, who was destined to emerge as one of the greatest thinkers in modern history.

William had a particularly difficult time getting a firm hold on life. After a brief stint as an artist, he knew he had to pick a more conventional career. His father's example gave him little help. Henry James had formulated grandiose metaphysical theories that seemingly explained the entire universe. Yet William was unable to deduce from these elaborate schemes any one direction that he should follow. He was an especially sensitive young man and soon began to crumble under the weight of trying to know with certainty what one, true vocation he should pursue. He developed nervous disorders that were to plague him the rest of his life. Chronic insomnia, eye trouble, digestive problems, and back pains were cruel reminders that his

upbringing had done little to help him come to grips with the real tasks of life. He had no direction in life, and his despair continued to worsen. He yearned for religious relief. However, his intellectual background made it impossible for him to believe in the divinity of Jesus, in the revealed origins of the Bible, or that any one religion has a monopoly on truth. He had, furthermore, long ago ceased believing in a God "up there" who hears our prayers and who occasionally chooses to intervene miraculously on our behalf.

William James was in many ways a prototype of modern individuals who yearn for a grand spiritual dimension to their lives yet feel alienated from conventional religious belief. He was destined to have to fight his way to an original religious outlook that moved beyond— rather than ignored—modern intellectual difficulties with organized religion. Only gradually was he able to assemble a spiritual philosophy that helped him restore his sense of personal vitality. In a manner similar to what psychologist Erik Erikson observed in Martin Luther, William James was able "to lift his individual patienthood to the level of a universal one and try to solve for all what he could not solve for himself."[3]

The first step toward regaining personal vitality was his humble recognition that "if we have to give up all hope of [depending on God] as vain and leading to nothing for us, then the only thing left to us is will."[4] James was trying to understand religion in a way that didn't make him a helpless victim, waiting—probably forever—for a supernatural being to rescue him. He demanded a religious humanism, that is, a religious outlook that focused only on those ideas that humans can know in full intellectual honesty and on what they can achieve through their own mental and emotional abilities.

During this period James wrote in his diary that his "strongest moral and intellectual craving is for some stable reality to lean upon."[5] Having found metaphysical speculation lacking in this regard, he turned instead to scientific thought. He vowed to rely on his own will power. He was thus trying to forge a purely secular orientation to life, guided by the kind of precise information afforded by reason and empirical investigation. William buried himself in the

William James (pfMS AM 1092; by permission of the Houghton Library, Harvard University)

study of the natural sciences, eventually earning a medical degree from Harvard University, and then joined its faculty to teach physiology. A few years later he opened up a laboratory for the study of psychology. Science, however, bored William. Much like John Muir, he found technical modes of thought too restrictive. Now that he had secured a more stable reality to lean on, he found himself yearning to recapture some of his father's awe-inspiring spirituality. And as fate was to have it, James accidentally happened upon one of the three experiences of wonder that were to redirect his life and thought.

While strolling through his laboratory one day, William spontaneously decided that it was time for him to discover firsthand what effect nitrous oxide has on the human nervous system. He had learned about nitrous oxide a few years before while reading an amateur philosopher's book titled *The Anaesthetic Revelation and the Gist of Philosophy*. The author, Paul Blood, was convinced that nitrous oxide leads to a striking epiphany: "The kingdom of God is . . . within you."[6] James considered himself a thoroughgoing empiricist. This meant that all ideas must be tested by experience. So, with respect to Blood's mystical claims, he had little recourse but to experiment for himself. The results were impressive. He had the experience of discovering "depth beyond depth of truth" and became convinced that there is a "profound meaning" to life that exists at an order of existence just beyond the scope of our physical senses. He concluded that although the effects will vary from person to person, there is a general pattern to the subjective effects of nitrous oxide: "With me, as with every other person of whom I have heard, the keynote of the experience is the tremendously exciting sense of an intense metaphysical illumination."[7]

This "metaphysical illumination" was a transformative moment in James's personal and professional life.[8] For one thing, nitrous oxide afforded him the chance to view religion from the "inside." From that moment forward he was able to appreciate the mystical experience from the mystic's own standpoint. More important, however, this wondrous experience provided James with an experiential context for his emerging interest in the philosophical concepts he

called "pluralism" and "radical empiricism." By pluralism James meant that there are always alternative points of view and that no one point of view is inherently privileged over others. Pluralism, however, went beyond this simple statement of philosophical tolerance: it was a full-fledged commitment to the possibility that there is no single, absolute truth. In this sense James was moving beyond scientism and to what is often called the "postmodern" view that focuses on how humans construct their various interpretations of reality. James's radical empiricism was also connected with the metaphysical illumination afforded by his experiment with nitrous oxide. James was convinced that experiences such as his and Blood's deserved to be considered authentic perceptions of reality. What the natural sciences ordinarily mean by empiricism is not fully empirical in that they typically restrict their understanding of experience to the normal waking state of consciousness. A radical empiricism is one that pays attention to the full range of human experience, including the kinds of mystical and religious experience that occur at the margins of waking consciousness.

A second wonder-filled experience reinforced the noetic force of his experience with nitrous oxide. James's concern with steering a middle path between scientific materialism and biblical religion prompted him to join the American branch of the Society for Psychical Research. He devoted a considerable amount of time and energy investigating alleged instances of spirit communication, telepathy, and clairvoyance. Any genuine instance of the paranormal was, to him, an event capable of evoking awe or wonder. He believed that even a single confirmed case of paranormal activity would be sufficient to show the limitations of modern science and force even the toughest-minded intellectual to acknowledge the existence of something "more" than physical reality. As he put it, "If you wish to upset the law that all crows are black, you mustn't seek to show that no crows are; it is enough if you prove one single crow to be white."[9] James was confident that he had come upon one such white crow. A trance medium by the name of Mrs. Lenora Piper was able to give him information that he was certain could not have been obtained

through fraud or deceit. Here was a full-blown experience of something that could not be expected within the framework of scientific rationality. It set his head spinning in pursuit of a metaphysical explanation. He realized that he could never be certain that Mrs. Piper received the information from a spirit, as she claimed. There were other possible explanations. For example, she might have gotten this information through telepathy or some other form of extrasensory perception. The incident was nonetheless critical to his eventual journey back to an essentially religious outlook on life. He now had another experiential template for believing that there was indeed something "more" to the universe beyond what could be objectively measured.

Some years later James had a distinct third experience dominated by the emotion of wonder. On a hiking and camping trip in the Adirondacks during the summer of 1898, James became exhausted from overexertion. That evening turned out to be one of the most memorable of his life. Having "got into a state of spiritual alertness of the most vivid description," James later struggled to find words that could describe his encounter with unexpected realities.

> I spent a good deal of [the night] in the woods where the streaming moonlight lit up things in a magical checkered play, and it seemed as if the gods of all the nature-mythologies were holding an indescribable meeting in my breast with the moral gods of the inner life. The two kinds of gods have nothing in common . . . [this imagery had an] intense significance of some sort, of the whole scene, if one could only tell the significance. . . . I can't find a single word for all that significance, and don't know what it was significant of, so there it remains a boulder of impression.[10]

During the experience James was aware that it in some way connected with the series of lectures he would soon deliver in Edinburgh, Scotland. As it turned out, the "boulder of impression" that lingered in his imagination would greatly influence these lectures on the varieties of religious experience. The experience made him acutely aware of the difference between a moral and a religious orien-

tation to life. The latter, he explained, differs from the former by the total abandonment of self-effort and, in so doing, the discovery of a higher power capable of exerting regenerative effects on our life. Religion is characterized by a letting go. It takes the form of a receptive rather than an active orientation to the surrounding world. It is thus no surprise that James later noted that "it was one of the happiest lonesome nights of my existence, and I understand now what a poet is." James hereby rediscovered the central truth of his father's Swedenborgian faith: that the highest forms of wholeness, meaning, and personal power are to be had by opening ourselves to an "influx" of spiritual energies that come to us from without.

Spirituality in an Unfinished Universe

The developed fruits of James's wondrous experiences can be seen in his epochal *The Varieties of Religious Experience*. First published in 1902, the *Varieties* argues that personal, mystical experience is the core of authentic religion. All the various creeds and rituals associated with the world's organized religions are, in James's view, but second-hand translations of the original mystical experiences from which they arose. Authentic spirituality is rooted in experiences that provide individuals with the felt conviction (1) that the visible world is part of a more spiritual universe from which it draws its chief significance and (2) that union or harmonious relation with that higher universe is our true end. Importantly, James's understanding of the authentic core of religion was at least partially anchored in his own earlier experiment with nitrous oxide: "Some years ago I myself made some observations on this aspect of nitrous oxide intoxication, and reported them in print. One conclusion was forced upon my mind at that time, and my impression of its truth has ever since remained unshaken. It is that our normal waking consciousness, rational consciousness as we call it, is but one special type of consciousness, whilst all about it, parted from it by the filmiest of screens, there lie potential forms of consciousness entirely different."[11]

James believed that these other "forms of consciousness" held the

key to understanding how one might steer a middle course between scientific materialism and conventional religiosity. Science, narrowly conceived, fails to understand that element within human nature that defies reduction to the language of material and efficient causation. James believed that humanity's mystical experiences constitute recurring data that call scientism into question. His own wonder-filled experiences further convinced him "of the continuity of our consciousness with a wider spiritual universe from which the ordinary person (who is the only person that scientific psychology, so called, takes cognizance of) is shut off."[12]

Although James was convinced that human consciousness was capable of connecting with something that is ontologically "more," he was just as wary of organized religion as he was of conventional science. He knew that for most people religion "has been made for them by others, communicated to them by tradition, determined to fixed forms by imitation, and retained by habit."[13] In short, religion consists largely of lifeless dogma maintained through group consensus and social reinforcement. Most religious beliefs are, in James's opinion, colored by irrationality, superstition, and sectarian intolerance. Furthermore, religious faith in the existence of a transcendent God who will someday act decisively to restore the world to his divine plan tends to foster moral irresponsibility. That is, religion tends to lull people into dependency and distracts them from assuming responsibility for the consequences of their actions. If forced to pick between religion and science, James would certainly have championed science as the better means of steering humans toward a productive relationship with the universe.

It was against both churched religion and conventional science that James proposed the possibility of being spiritual in a coscientific way. For James, religion really wasn't about beliefs. It was about experience—the experience of opening up to a "spiritual more" at the fringes of everyday consciousness. It is, James proclaimed, only by letting go of ego-dominated rationality that we put ourselves in a position to experience otherwise unexpected phenomena: "There are resources in us that naturalism with its literal and legal virtues

never recks of, possibilities that take our breath away, of another kind of happiness and power, based on giving up our own will and letting something higher work for us, and these seem to show a world wider than either physics or philistine ethics can imagine."[14]

Spirituality, for James, was about cultivating states of awareness that "take our breath away" and produce a qualitatively different "kind of happiness and power." Spirituality was thus something fraught with wonder. It is triggered by the sudden perception of a causal presence that is somehow "more" than the material order of things. It brings joy. It heightens interest in the world. It makes us capable of sustained action on behalf of the wider universe with which we now know ourselves to be intimately connected. It lures us out of our egocentric orientation to experience and enables us to see more fully the needs and interests of other organisms, including those whose lives are very different than our own.[15] In this way, spiritual states of awareness mobilize energetic action on behalf of other living organisms.

James's own wonder-filled experiences "forced upon his mind" a fresh perspective on life. They afforded him what De Pascuale calls a mindful awareness of the world. And, as De Pascuale contends, these distinctive modes of apprehending the world afforded James the possibility of choosing *how* to be, as well as what it means to become a true individual and a true citizen of the universe. In James's case, this meant choosing to be a citizen of an evolving, unfinished universe. James's vision of an evolving universe underscored the importance of moral conduct. In an unfinished universe there can be real gains and losses. The final outcome will depend on our actions. In a very real sense, then, we and God (i.e., the ultimate causal power responsible for all world-building and wholeness-making activity in the world) have business with each other. It is true that wonder-filled states make us receptive to a higher causal order of life. As James put it, they show us that "we inhabit an invisible spiritual environment from which help comes, our soul being mysteriously one with a larger soul whose instruments we are."[16] The future, nonetheless, is still up for grabs. We are the "instruments" through which the higher

powers of life might work to strengthen life and create wholeness. The final outcome is therefore dependent on the vitality and appropriateness of our worldly actions.

By building on his own experiences of continuity with a "more," James was able to extend empiricism to include humanity's moral and religious experience. He also redefined spirituality in such a way that it rested on the cultivation of certain wonder-charged states of awareness rather than on membership in a formal religious institution. And, in so doing, James carved out a kind of middle ground between scientific positivism and revealed religion. Both psychologists and theologians have faulted James for lingering in this middle ground and never embracing either of their intellectual commitments. But, as Carol Zaleski has remarked, it was James who kept the door to religion open when the reigning scientific method kept trying to slam it shut for all those who wish to build their personal worldviews in connection with reason and scientific discovery. And it was James who kept the door open to a form of "religion without revelation" when the nation's churches kept trying to slam it shut for unchurched seekers. Zaleski concludes that for many of us "there is still need of James's door-holding services."[17] Indeed, many of our contemporaries are in vital need of wondrous experiences that, when attended to, might give birth to self-examination and a mindful awareness of the world.

6. Wonder and Psychological Development

Those who wonder discover that this in itself is wonder.
—M. C. ESCHER

T HE NATURAL SCIENCES HAVE MADE IMPORTANT CONTRI-
butions to our understanding of the experience of wonder.
Biologically we know that humans are genetically designed
to respond to unexpected features of the environment in ways that
ensure survival and promote our general well-being. Emotions guide
this adaptive process by mobilizing perception and cognition in ways
that serve our vital needs and interests. It seems, however, that different emotions serve very different sets of needs and interests. A life
shaped by wonder is thus one characterized by needs and interests
unlike those pursued by people whose lives are relatively devoid of
this emotional sensibility.

The life of William James illustrates how experiences of wonder
orient us to very particular kinds of needs and interests. Trained at
Harvard in the natural sciences, James became singularly uninterested
in the kinds of reductionistic thinking that characterized the science of
his day. His greater need was to understand how our lives fit into some
larger cosmic whole. Both his psychological and philosophical writings are characterized by their heuristic or open-ended quality. Thus

James's life and thought, much like those of John Muir, demonstrate how certain experiences of wonder direct attention beyond the immediate environment to a more general level of existence. Neither Muir nor James possessed the cognitive temperament for sustained interest in the particulars of life. Nor were they especially concerned with curiosity-driven manipulation of things or with solving problems that might yield utilitarian results (though Muir, before his sustained exposure to the "Godful beauty" of nature, was quite successful as an inventor). With the passage of time both became ever more disposed toward the fairly passive contemplation of why things are as they are. Their lives thus provide partial support of the view that experiences of wonder shape our personal lives in quite distinctive ways. Such experiences bring different needs and interests to the fore, thereby altering the course of personal development. And for this reason the discipline of developmental psychology is also in a position to contribute to our understanding of the "prototypical characteristics" of the experience of wonder.

The Course of Cognitive Development

Wonder, like all emotional experiences, has cognitive elements. It presupposes a discrepancy between previous cognitive expectations and some new event. This discrepancy produces the "astonishment mingled with perplexity or bewildered curiosity" that defines wonder. As an emotional response to unexpected stimuli, wonder prompts us to abandon earlier cognitive structures and develop new ones that might better account for these unexpected perceptions. It follows that wonder is a critical element of cognitive development over the course of the human life span.

Wonder promotes adaptation by stimulating the association cortex, compelling the creation of new, more expansive "interpretive" categories. In particular, it motivates us to construct ever more general understandings of reality that might account for the causal source of unexpected stimuli. Put differently, wonder prompts us to think in more abstract (rather than concrete) terms. The human

capacity for such abstract thought is intimately linked with the co-evolution of our larger cerebral cortex and our cultural mode of existence. As Aristotle noted, "The animals other than humans live by appearances and memories, and have but little of connected experience; but the human race lives also by art and reasonings."[1] Such reasonings, according to Aristotle, include contemplation of the ultimate cause, meaning, and intentionality of "being" in general. That is, humanity's highest cognitive achievements have a decidedly metaphysical quality in that they require the construction of mental categories that go beyond what is "out there" in the physical world. Wonder, by stimulating the formation of higher-level categories of thought, is a principal source of such distinctively metaphysical modes of cognition.

A better understanding of the role that wonder plays in the course of cognitive development can be found by reviewing the research of the Swiss psychological theorist Jean Piaget. Trained in zoology, Piaget hoped to develop a broadly biological explanation of the process through which humans gradually construct knowledge.[2] He closely observed children, particularly his own children, as they learned to make sense of the world about them. Of particular interest to Piaget was the sequential process through which children come to understand such things as causality, the relationship between parts and wholes, and the relationship between change and constancy. He eventually identified three distinct phases in the normal course of cognitive development: the sensorimotor phase (roughly, from birth to age two), during which infants relate to the world largely through reflexes and acquired motor habits; the phase of "concrete operations" (roughly, ages two to eleven), during which young children learn to organize experience into fairly static configurations; and the phase of "formal operations" (beginning after the age of twelve), when teens gradually learn to construct hypothetical models of reality that allow them to consider and compare ideas and thereby achieve a measure of mental control or direction over their lives. Subsequent researchers have challenged Piaget's argument concerning the universality of these phases and his relative neglect of the role

that environmental conditions play in the way that children learn to construct their reality. Nonetheless, Piaget's essential paradigms have generated the bulk of what we know today about cognitive development and provide a helpful context for understanding how the emotional experience of wonder contributes to acquisition of specific kinds of cognitive skills.[3]

Piaget studied the way that children tried to solve various problems that arose while interacting with their natural and social environments. Each new problem disrupted the equilibrium that had previously existed between children and their world, thereby motivating them to acquire new cognitive understandings that would once again allow them to interact successfully with their surroundings. Piaget was thus interpreting cognitive development as a form of biological adaptation. He found it useful to explain this ongoing process of adaptation by drawing attention to the two alternating ways that we relate to our world: assimilation and accommodation. Assimilation represents our efforts to incorporate new experiences into the existing stock of ideas with which we fashion our goal-seeking behavior. When a new experience can't be assimilated into existing cognitive schemata, accommodation occurs. Accommodation refers to changes the individual makes to adjust to the environment. Accommodation signifies the way we modify our previous cognitive structures to include those new features of the environment learned through new or unexpected perceptions.

It is easy to see why surprise, curiosity, and wonder exert critical influences on the overall course of cognitive development. All three emotions originate as reactions to unexpected events, mobilizing efforts to change cognitive structures in ways that will ensure our overall well-being. Surprise is the most general of these "orienting responses" and may easily combine with curiosity or wonder. William Charlesworth points out that Piaget's entire model of cognitive development hinges around the central role played by the emotion of surprise. Charlesworth explains that surprise is a complex orienting response that has an "instigatory effect on attentional and curiosity behaviors" needed if unexpected "stimuli are to become

part of and help reshape existing cognitive schemata."[4] Surprise is an emotional system that has a general arousal effect. Surprise mobilizes selective attention to the environment and thereby alters our manner of attending to, and processing, sensory information. Surprise thus ensures that the organism behaves in such a way as to produce new knowledge about problematic properties of the environment. And, in so doing, surprise triggers higher-level thinking: "Under normal environmental conditions surprise reaction and subsequent attentional and curiosity behaviors are very hard to suppress, and for this reason they seem to be good candidates for the mechanisms that insure that most individuals make the progression from sensorimotor intelligence to formal thought."[5]

Piaget was also aware that curiosity, like surprise, motivates cognitive growth. He frequently observed how curiosity propels children to interact proactively with their environment. Piaget often used the metaphor of "little scientists" to capture the way that curiosity drives children to investigate and create in the context of their investigations of the world. His point was that curiosity is rewarding in its own right. Curiosity draws children into sustained rapport with their environment. Curiosity motivates children not just to register experience passively but to organize and interpret such experience. Of special significance is the fact that curiosity motivates sustained investigation of the relationship between ideas and experience. Curiosity therefore helps individuals refine their conceptions of the world to correspond more closely with the actual facts of experience.

Piaget's research focused primarily on the developmental acquisition of what is commonly referred to as domain-specific knowledge. That is, Piaget studied the gradual acquisition of knowledge related to very specific mental operations (e.g., the development of specific concepts such as causality, change vs. constancy, or the relationship between parts and wholes). Only rarely did Piaget concern himself with the ability to think in ways that stretch beyond specific domains. Thus Piaget, and developmental psychologists in general, extolled the role of curiosity in fostering the assimilation of environmental patterns into our working stock of ideas, but they inadvertently de-

flected scientific attention away from cognitive activities that seek to make connections between different kinds of things or to put things together in higher-order ways. And these, of course, are the cognitive activities most directly stimulated by the emotion of wonder.

Fortunately, the total context of Piaget's work provides helpful insights concerning how wonder leads to the development of higher-order or metaphysical forms of thought. In his *The Language and Thought of the Child*, Piaget noted that the emergence of "why" questions in early childhood is linked with the first appearance of more abstract cognitive structures. Children seem to delight in contemplating just why things are as they are. This continuous inquiry into "why" things appear as they do reveals that children are naturally curious about the purposes, intentionality, or teleology of things. As children contemplate why life appears as it does, they have a natural tendency to infer the existence of a reality that in some way lies beyond or behind observed reality. Belief in the existence of an imperceptible reality behind the world of appearances enables children to entertain concepts of what might unite objects or what might give them their purpose or meaning.

This is an important observation. Children seek not only to understand immediate causal mechanisms but also to understand them in terms of some broader framework. This begins fairly early in childhood when children ponder such intangible matters as what the world was like before they were born, what life was like in the time of dinosaurs, or what life will be like when they grow up.[6] All such cognitive operations require children to construct larger contexts based on nonactual, fictional, and metaphysical possibilities of the past, present, or future. This capacity to think in terms of possibilities forms the earliest foundations of the eventual movement from "concrete operations" to "formal operational thought" during adolescence. Formal operational thought requires the ability to entertain abstract, possible constructions of reality. These abstract mental constructs guide hypothetico-deductive reasoning through which we conceive and compare alternative behavioral strategies. Thus, as Piaget notes, the adolescent differs from the child by becoming "an

individual who thinks beyond the present and forms theories about everything, delighting especially in considerations of that which is not."[7] The highest levels of reasoning require the construction of a hypothetical model of existence, a structured whole that can be used to assess the meaning or value of the observed particulars of life. As Piaget states, at this important stage "reality becomes secondary to possibility."[8] The existence of higher-order conceptions of reality frees us from sheer necessity and brute survival to consider a wide variety of existential and ethical orientations to life.

My point here is that just as curiosity propels children to sustain their inquiries into the workings of physical reality, wonder is a prime motivational force in the emergence of higher-order conceptions of existence. Wonder disrupts equilibrium and prompts us to accommodate to the most general order of thinking possible—an order from which we might contemplate the intrinsic cause or intentionality of things. Wonder-driven thinking serves needs and interests that vary considerably from those pertaining to the tasks of hunting and gathering. These needs and interests have less to do with the assimilation of new action-oriented schemata into our cognitive repertoire than with accommodating ourselves to a wider universe. Wonder is therefore geared toward the kind of "art and reasonings" that Aristotle described as distinctive to human beings.

Wonder plays a critical role in prompting the progression from concrete operations to formal operational thought. It encourages the construction of hypothetical or possible orders of existence that might causally account for unexpected perceptions. Wonder is thus one of the major sources of our capacity to entertain the possible. Neither children nor adults have, at least in principle, any problem distinguishing between the actual and the possible. The difficulty lies instead in discerning the boundaries of the possible.[9] We lack any means of empirically testing our conceptions of the possible. For this reason we typically rely on our own intuitive sense of plausibility and, of course, on the mythic and theological traditions of our community. Beginning with Piaget, developmental psychologists have implicitly denigrated such possibility-driven thought owing to its

frequent connection with superstition and irrationality. Developmental psychologists have implicitly favored cognitive processes associated with assimilation (which can be empirically tested in ongoing experience and hence often move toward increased objectivity and verification) rather than those associated with accommodation (which are not always susceptible to such empirical testing).[10]

This unfortunate slighting of the role of wonder by cognitive psychologists is especially curious given the role it played in Piaget's own life and thought. In young adulthood he had already become expert at the technical reasoning skills then associated with scientific biology. Piaget's godfather was concerned that his mind was becoming too narrow and decided to introduce him to the writings of the French philosopher Henri Bergson. Bergson viewed nature in mystically charged ways. His concepts of "creative evolution" and of the presence of "the élan vital" throughout nature lured the young Piaget into considering how the observable universe might participate in a grander metaphysical order of things. Bergson's writings opened up the budding scientist's sense of wonder. The intellectual experience, he recounted, was "a moment of enthusiasm close to ecstatic joy."[11] This newfound ability to perceive a divine presence within nature changed his entire life. He claimed to have been "seized by the demon of reflection" and realized that the study of natural growth and development was simultaneously the study of how a divine spirit progressively manifests itself through our lives.[12]

Piaget's wondrous intellectual breakthrough gave him an experiential template for understanding how older, narrower cognitive structures can be disrupted, prompting us to accommodate our minds to a more inclusive sense of reality. Bergson's writings evoked a fantastic vision of the possibility that all developmental processes throughout nature are but the mechanisms through which an immanent spiritual force progressively strives toward some "supreme" or "ideal" telos. Thus, in his autobiography, Piaget defined beauty as "the love the individual feels for the ideal equilibrium" and explained that nature has an inherent urge to evolve toward "the ultimate order of the universe."[13] This metaphysical vision also enabled Piaget to

circumvent the traditional impasse between religion and science. He was able to envision science—like nature itself—as the divine made manifest. He could therefore focus his professional work on narrow questions concerning cognitive development confident that at the same time he was revealing the great mysteries of how God creates a universe. Piaget never engaged in metaphysics in a formal sense. But the personal meaning or purpose of his lifework flowed from the wonder inspired by his perception that something ideal was manifesting itself in the developmental processes of life. The ultimate meaning of life was to be found not by dissecting the many parts of life but by finally seeing how these parts relate to the "ultimate order of the universe."

As seen in Piaget's life and work, the course of cognitive development entails much more than the acquisition of skills for manipulating our external environment. Children are also curious in their own right, eager to accommodate to features of the environment that arouse their interest and that disclose something that strikes them as intensely powerful, real, true, or beautiful. That is, they find themselves moved by wonder to approach and make contact with the surrounding world. They derive pleasure not only from discovering discrete objects but also from discovering "something more," some greater whole that connects and imparts meaning to otherwise separate objects. Wonder elicits sustained accommodation to the widest possible range of human experience even as it triggers the construction of cognitive categories that make it possible to seek what Aristotle described as "final" rather than "efficient" or "material" causes of human well-being.

Connecting Self and World

In recent years a number of psychologists have drawn attention to the importance of interpersonal relationships in psychological development. These psychologists, often referred to as "self psychologists" or "object relations" theorists, argue that interpersonal relationships are the key medium through which the human self develops.[14] This

view is in sharp contrast to Sigmund Freud's basic paradigm for understanding psychological development. Freud focused more narrowly on dynamic processes occurring within the individual. In his view personal identity develops as a by-product of the individual's ongoing struggle to regulate his or her instinctual demands. For Freud, personal integration is achieved to the degree that the rational ego successfully regulates instinctual gratification within the context of social or moral demands imposed from without.

Subsequent theorists who otherwise share Freud's basic insights have subordinated the role that instinctual dynamics play in the development of our sense of personal identity. They have instead focused on how our sense of personal identity emerges through the medium of interpersonal relationships. Erik Erikson, Heinz Kohut, Melanie Klein, D. W. Winnicott, and Henry Guntrip are among those who have examined the role that personal relationships play in the gradual evolution of the self. They have shown that achieving a strong and cohesive sense of self requires very particular kinds of relationships capable of supporting psychological health. These relationships enable us to acquire a sense of being prized or valued individuals while yet understanding ourselves as autonomous and morally responsible. As Henry Guntrip summarized this view, "for good or ill, the universe has begotten us with an absolute need to be able to relate in fully personal terms to an environment that we feel relates beneficially to us."[15] If we are to grow and develop as individuals, we need to feel that we are intimately related to a world that values us as individuals.

Heinz Kohut drew on his therapeutic experience to explain how optimal psychological development requires the continuing presence of other people who make it possible for us to sustain the two psychological functions he termed "mirroring" and "idealization."[16] The mirroring response first occurs when the infant feels her or his worth mirrored back from the face of a nurturing parent. Finding our self-worth mirrored back to us from a valued "other" makes it possible to develop a sense of vitality, cohesiveness, and goodness. Idealization occurs as the self comes to feel connected or attached to a

grander being. This grander being might be an admired parent, a family, a school, a nation, or a supernatural being such as God. To the extent that a person can feel connected to such a valued "higher being," he or she receives a sense of purpose or meaningfulness.

The quality of psychological development over the course of life is greatly affected by the continuing presence of relationships that permit both mirroring and idealization. We are motivated to seek out and even create modes of relationship that can help us feel vital, integrated, and connected to higher meanings. This quest to engage the world in ways that support psychological health begins in early childhood with the emergence of our capacities for play and imagination. Children learn to relate to the world through fantasy or imagination. Fantasy and imagination blur any sharp distinction between internal and external reality. Playful thinking creates a kind of intermediate space that offers a safe transition between self and world. D. W. Winnicott referred to this as "transitional space" that provides a safe, inviting space between children and their surroundings. Winnicott also noted how some objects such as a doll, a teddy bear, or an imaginary friend come to be "transitional objects" that make it possible for children to feel safe when interacting with the surrounding world. As Winnicott notes, the transitional space created through play and fantasy continues throughout life and makes possible our engagement with the arts, religion, imaginative living, and creative scientific work.[17]

The point here is that there are psychological reasons why our capacity for creatively engaging the world depends on our ability to establish relationships that support important needs. In particular, we need to be able to relate to life in ways that meet our needs for mirroring (having a sense of intrinsic worth communicated to us) and idealization (feeling connected to a "higher" purpose of meaning). We also need to relate to life in ways that make it safe and inviting for us to reach out and make contributions to the surrounding world. Psychoanalyst Ana-Marie Rizzuto studies how religious beliefs have traditionally met these important psychological needs. She observes that children initially create transitional space through

a variety of magical and fantasy-laden ways of constructing their world. Heroes, imaginary friends, fairy tale characters, angels, and saints all create transitional space that help children continue to feel safe even as they become more separated and distanced from the nurturing parent. The relationship a child establishes with these transitional objects helps her or him tolerate unavoidable experiences of frustration or inadequacy. As these initial imaginary objects gradually lose their power, the concept of God emerges to create a more stable notion of a valued "higher power" with whom one might sustain an intimate relationship. Unlike other transitional objects, the concept of God is supported by the culture's official values, strivings, and aspirations. God is a shared "transitional object." The symbol of God shapes an ontological reality for all those who live within its symbolic reach. The concept of God, according to Rizzuto, is much more than an illusion: "It is an integral part of being human, truly human in our *capacity to create nonvisible but meaningful realities* capable of containing our potential for imaginative expansion beyond the boundaries of our senses."[18]

This need to engage "nonvisible but meaningful realities" is a key to understanding how the emotion of wonder nourishes psychological health over the course of our personal lives. Wonder transforms our experience of the world in ways that support our ongoing need for idealization. That is, wonder imbues the world with a "luring" quality with which we feel intimately connected. It also motivates sustained engagement or participation in activities that seemingly move us closer toward such nonvisible but meaningful orders of life. Wonder thus reconfigures perception and cognition in ways that address what Guntrip described as our "absolute need to be able to relate in fully personal terms to an environment that we feel relates beneficially to us."

Because wonder encourages us to think beyond the ordinary boundaries of understanding, it frequently leads to both fantasy and magical thinking. It might, for example, prompt us to posit the existence of supernatural beings such as fairies, angels, or gods. It might also encourage magical forms of thinking that blur accustomed

boundaries between internal and external realities. While such beliefs might not be "true" in the sense of being propositions of fact, they render the world in ways that are conducive to psychological well-being. Wondrous beliefs provide a sense of connection with or participation in the wider environment. They foster a sense of being intimately connected to "higher realities" teeming with meaning and significance. They also configure the world in such a way as to make it appear responsive to our personal will and our innermost desires.

The fantastical and magical elements of wonder-driven thinking can, of course, lead to narcissistic pathology in which the world becomes nothing more than an extension of one's own needs and interests. Wonder-born cognition can lead us away from productive relations with reality if is fully severed from environmental feedback and critical reflection. But this is not to say that the metaphysical constructions to which wonder often leads are nothing more than delusions. The ability to envisage "nonvisible but meaningful realities" is a prerequisite to humanity's greatest accomplishments (e.g., the conception of universal human rights, visions of social justice, commitment to the intrinsic worth of future generations and the ecological claims they put on us). It is this capacity to envision a more general order of existence that makes it possible for us conceptualize our world as a universe rather than a pluriverse. It also makes it possible to speak of intrinsic meanings and values. It is the function of wonder, then, to shape our conception of the universe in a way that invites our spirited engagement. Wonder is thus potentially not less than rational but rather more than rational. The psychologist and philosopher William James once observed that the most rational construction of the universe is one that includes a felt sense of the presence and causal influence of "something more." In James's opinion it is just such a sense of the reality of the seen that renders the world eminently conducive to the full development of humanity's creative powers: "Not an energy of our active nature to which it does not authoritatively appeal, not an emotion of which it does not normally and naturally release the springs. At a single stroke, it changes the dead blank *it* of the world into a living *thou*, with whom the

whole man may have dealings."[19] Any emotion capable of evoking vivid experiences of "something more" and thereby transforming the world into a living "thou" must be considered among the most critical ingredients of full psychological and moral well-being.

Wonder, Empathy, and Care

Wonder, by helping us to feel connected with "something more," transforms our world into a living "thou" that invites our full participation. Wonder is thus one of the emotions that motivate some of humanity's highest developmental achievements. Both John Muir and William James demonstrate how full psychological development requires more than the acquisition of rational, problem-solving skills. It also requires the ability to engage any number of "nonvisible but meaningful realities" that hold the key to our long-term fulfillment—both as individuals and as a species. For both Muir and James, it was the experience of wonder that reconfigured their perception of the world in such a way as to lead beyond ethical egoism to what De Pascuale calls "a mindful awareness of the world." They were able to identify profoundly with needs and interests that most of us find remote and incapable of eliciting our interest. For both Muir and James, wonder proved powerful enough to see themselves as true citizens of the universe.

A possible clue to the role that wonder might play in the development of high-level moral thinking can be found in the work of developmental psychologist Lawrence Kohlberg. Kohlberg devoted the bulk of his career to studying the acquisition of moral thinking skills. He observed that adulthood raises profound questions concerning whether it really "pays" to try to be moral. Responsibility for the sustained care of others requires us to make ongoing decisions about how best to care for others. With this comes the realization that there really aren't any perfect moral answers "out there" for us but that instead we largely create the world through our own decisions and values. If it is really we who engender an order onto life by the values we choose, then which values should we teach the young? Sustained

responsibility for others raises an even more unsettling question: Why bother to stand for any set of moral obligations if it is indeed possible that the universe is either indifferent or perhaps even hostile to our moral efforts? Kohlberg found that even those people who had previously acquired well-developed ethical standards frequently face skepticism concerning why, in a universe that is largely unjust, we should commit ourselves to moral principles rather than just look out for ourselves. He discovered that in midlife "the answer to the question 'Why be moral?' at this level entails the question 'Why live?' (and the parallel question, 'How face death?') so that ultimate moral maturity requires a mature solution to the question of the meaning of life. This, in turn, is hardly a moral question per se; it is an ontological or a religious one. Not only is the question not a moral one but it is not a question resolvable on purely logical or rational grounds as moral questions are."[20]

Sustained responsibility for our own and others' lives finally prompts us to contemplate our place in the greater scheme of things. What is at question here is not our rational capacity to codify ethical principles but our capacity to feel intimately connected to meanings that can be affirmed as intrinsic to life. The highest levels of moral understanding thus depend on our capacity to move beyond logical or rational constructions of the world. Kohlberg concluded that being able to grasp the ultimate reason for caring (the ultimate reason for living) requires the ability to enter occasionally into states that the philosopher Spinoza described as "the union of the mind with the whole frame of nature." Kohlberg wrote, "The logic of such experience is sometimes expressed in theistic terms, but it need not be. Its essential is the sense of being a part of the whole of life and the adoption of a cosmic, as opposed to a [purely rationalistic] perspective."[21] It entails, in other words, the capacity to engage nonvisible but meaningful orders of reality.

An essential task required of us in adult life, then, is that of at least occasionally moving beyond sheer egoism and adopting a cosmic perspective on life. Moreover, it seems that evolution selected for organisms whose emotional systems enable them to accomplish pre-

cisely this. Emotions motivate both our perceptual and cognitive systems to assign meaning and value to experiences such that we might respond properly to environmental situations. The emotion of wonder has been "selected for" over the course of our evolutionary history at least in part owing to its capacity to motivate perception and cognition in ways that bolster our capacities for both mutuality and care. According to ethical theorist Martha Nussbaum, it is the emotion of wonder that is most responsible for our emerging capacities for love, empathy, and compassion. Wonder, she writes, is the emotion that responds "to the pull of the object, and one might say that in it the subject is maximally aware of the value of the object, and only minimally aware, if at all, of its relationship to her own plans. That is why it is likely to issue in contemplation, rather than in any other sort of action toward the object."[22]

Nussbaum suggests that wonder is the emotion that most clearly enables humans to move beyond self-interest to recognize and respond to others in their own right. Insofar as people remain bound by ego-centered perspectives of the world, their ethical orientation is largely eudaemonistic (i.e., geared toward personal well-being as regulated by rational calculations of self-interest). Yet "wonder, as non-eudaemonistic as an emotion can be, helps move distant objects within the circle of a person's scheme of ends . . . seeing others as part of one's own circle of concern."[23] It is, then, the emotion of wonder that most readily enables us to become capable of true empathy or compassion. The very existence of living beings who appear to us as an ultimate limit to our own egoism awakens wonder at the way in which others embody the ultimate source of all life and vitality. As Nussbaum observes, "wonder at the complex living thing itself" is what mobilizes our compassion and empathy. Wonder redraws our world of concern, establishing true mutuality with a wider sphere of life.

The capacity of wonder to develop our potential for mutuality, empathy, and care is also a key to what distinguishes some individuals as effective leaders. As Robert Greenleaf found in his study of leadership, the key to responsible action resides in "our capacity for

wonder." He discovered that "wonder is an attitude, it is the filter through which one perceives the world, a filter that tends to substitute moral concern for criticism. It prompts one to ask, 'What is going on here?' before one acts; and, though the provocation may be extreme, it leads to a response of thoughtfulness—even amusement, rather than of fear, anger, or dismay. It lifts one above the tumult and gives one perspective. And to wonder is humbling, it opens one to learn."[24]

Venturing Outward: Intrinsic Motivation

A recurring issue in psychological theory is how best to account for the tendency of many humans to explore their environment, seek out novelty, or proactively initiate contact with their surroundings. Accounting for such behavior is problematic within many of the theoretical orientations that dominate academic psychology. Psychoanalysis, for example, depicts humans as being at the mercy of instinctual urges and cultural constraints. Psychoanalysis assumes, moreover, that individuals are motivated to rid themselves of stimulation, seeking to return to a state of relative quiescence. In this view humans seek to avoid sustained engagement with the world, not seek it out. Behaviorist psychology, meanwhile, explains human behavior as wholly conditioned by the contingencies of reinforcement operating in the external environment. Behaviorists consequently depict humans as passive recipients of environmental conditioning. Like psychoanalysts, they envision human nature as embedded within larger forces that make it virtually impossible for them to initiate free or creative behavior.

It is for this reason that many psychologists have recently begun to pay attention to the way that emotions affect the human motivational system. Emotions regulate a host of psychological activities. They influence both perception and cognition by directing the way that we attend to, filter, and interpret environmental stimuli. Psychologist Carroll Izard notes that by regulating these perceptual and cognitive activities, "emotions constitute the primary motivational

system for human beings."[25] Izard considers it important to realize that while many emotions may indeed foster "embeddedness," other emotions seem to free us from either instinctual or environmental control. This is why Izard believes it important to differentiate closely between emotions. He maintains that by studying specific emotions, particularly the emotion of interest, we can shed important light on the psychological processes whereby individuals come to explore their environment, seek out novelty, or proactively initiate contact with their surroundings.

The emotion of interest, according to Izard and Ackerman, is the emotion closest to wonder in terms of its affect on motivation. They proceed to explain that both wonder and interest lie behind much of humanity's "urge to explore or discover": "Interest motivates exploration and learning, and guarantees the person's engagement in the environment. Survival and adaptation require such engagement. Interest supports creativity because it immerses one in the object or task and cues a sense of possibility. To paraphrase Tomkins (1962), interest is the only emotion that can sustain long-term constructive or creative endeavors."[26]

Izard and Ackerman note, furthermore, that the emotion of interest most typically occurs in a pattern with the emotion of joy. Sustained engagement with the environment therefore is typically experienced as intrinsically joyful or pleasurable. They suggest that wonder can be characterized as the coupling of joy and interest. Wonder, by making the urge to explore seem intrinsically joyful, supports "intrinsic motivation." That is, the motivational influence of joy and interest together makes engagement with the surrounding environment rewarding in its own right. This specific emotional state mobilizes us to seek out new experience and to engage in creative endeavors as intrinsically rewarding activities. Izard and Ackerman's research thus suggests that the emotion of wonder, like the emotion of interest, "animates and enlivens the mind and body . . . [and] provides the motivation and resources for constructive and creative endeavor, the development of intelligence, and personal growth."[27]

This linking of interest, joy, and wonder to "intrinsic motivation" has close parallels in both Abraham Maslow's and Ernest Schactel's work on the relationship between motivation and modes of perception. Maslow, former president of the American Psychological Association, is probably best known for his writings on peak experiences and the hierarchy of human needs. But among his most respected publications are those studying the connection between motivation and perceptual style. Maslow observed that we are motivated to meet needs. Basic needs (i.e., food, shelter, sex) are prepotent over "higher" needs (i.e., personal growth, creative expression, self-actualization). Maslow then suggested that there is a significant psychological difference "when persons are deficiency-need-gratification-bent and when they are growth-motivated or self-actualizing."[28] By this he meant that when people are principally motivated to meet basic needs, their perception and cognition have identifiable characteristics: sharp figure-ground differentiation, selective perception focused to reveal need-meeting characteristics of the environment, sensory stimuli organized and interpreted according to preformed cognitive sets, active or willful shaping of information by the perceiver, and attending to objects chiefly for their utilitarian value in meeting need. Such "deficiency-cognition" is most clearly seen in our relationships to others. When motivated by the need to gratify basic needs, we tend to view others not as wholes or unique individuals but rather from the perspective of their utility.

All of this is in contrast to the cognitive and perceptual style that emerges when we are relatively free from the motivating influence of basic-need gratification. What Maslow termed "Being-cognition" is also associated with certain perceptual characteristics: a tendency to see one's life in relation to the whole cosmos, relative blurring of the figure-ground relationship, more passive, and relatively purposeless in the sense of attending to unique characteristics of the environment regardless of immediate utility. Maslow also noticed that when cognition is free of the constraints imposed by our basic needs we become more capable of what he called an "aesthetic perception of the whole person . . . and furthermore approval, admiration, and love are

based less upon gratitude for usefulness and more upon the objective, intrinsic qualities of the perceived person."[29] Maslow further observed that this perception of intrinsic meanings and values is accompanied by "such emotions as *wonder*, awe, reverence, humility, and surrender."[30] Among the principal characteristics of this Being-cognition is that even mundane objects are often perceived as sacred, holy, "very special." When perceived in this way, the object "demands" or "calls for" awe, reverence, piety, *wonder*.[31]

Ernest Schactel similarly identified a particular mode of perception and cognition as the crucial variable affecting our capacity for constructive and creative endeavor. Schactel conceded that our ordinary mode of perceiving and conceptualizing the world perpetuates our fundamental embeddedness in instinctual drives and environmental conditioning. Schactel referred to this mode of perception and cognition as "autocentric" in that its motivation is to identify the utilitarian qualities of people or objects in our environment. Schactel pointed out, however, that we are also capable of what he called an "allocentric" (other-centered rather than self-centered) orientation to the world in which people or objects are attended to in their own fullness and richness. Every act of allocentric perception has an element of affirmation that acknowledges the object as existing in its own right. Attention to the fullness of the object rather than merely its need-meeting qualities "is characterized by an inexhaustible and ineffable quality, by the profoundest interest in the object, and by the enriching, refreshing, vitalizing effect which the act of perception has on the perceiver."[32] Such perceptual openness frees us from fixed anticipations and cognitive sets, making it possible for us to perceive the world in creatively new ways. Allocentric perception also drastically alters motivation. Rather than being motivated by instinctual demand or environmental forces, we find ourselves possessing "an insatiable curiosity and wish to approach and make contact with the surrounding world in a thousand different ways."[33]

Psychologists typically define human intelligence in terms of the efficiency with which we execute utilitarian tasks. It is quite possible, however, that fully allocentric perception reveals our potential for a

higher kind of intelligence. After all, if humanity's highest perceptual capacity "is that of allocentric interest to which the world never becomes a closed book, then the greater intelligence may be that which does not quickly dispose of or deal with an object but *wonders* at it and does not tire easily of contemplating and exploring it even if to others it may be the most familiar thing imaginable."[34]

Experiences of wonder—by triggering such allocentric perception—disclose the full range of our human potential. They reveal that we are motivated to do more than merely fulfill instinctual demands and comply with social reinforcement schemes. We are, it seems, also capable of continued growth and development throughout the course of our lives. While perceiving the world through the lens of wonder we transcend the object-of-use perspective and relate to others and to the world for the sake of the relationship itself.

7. A Life Shaped by Wonder: Rachel Carson

I should ask that the [good fairy's] gift to each child
in the world be a sense of wonder so indestructible that
it would last throughout life.—RACHEL CARSON

THE PREVIOUS CHAPTER REVIEWED WHAT DEVELOP-
mental psychology contributes to our understanding of
the prototypical characteristics of wonder. A life shaped by
wonder can be expected to reveal a number of clearly identifiable
intellectual and moral qualities. Wonder is, as we learned, among the
emotional experiences that help develop formal operational thought.
For this reason it is likely to lead to more abstract, higher-order conceptions of the world. Such thought is integral to the formation of
moral and religious understandings of our place in the greater scheme
of things. And, importantly, wonder lures us beyond self-centered
perspectives of the world and elicits our affective capacity for mutuality, empathy, and care. Perhaps more than any other emotional
experience, wonder draws us into sustained rapport with—and action on behalf of—the wider environment.

The experience of wonder first arises as an emotional episode of
relatively brief duration. But, like all other emotional experiences,
experiences of wonder also have the potential to shape longer-lasting

moods and personality traits. It thus makes sense to speak not only of experiences of wonder but also of an ongoing "sense of wonder." To better understand prototypical characteristics of such a sense of wonder, me might again avail ourselves of yet another exemplar of wonder—the environmental activist Rachel Carson. Just as with Muir and James, there is no pretense here that we are engaging in anything more than a cursory overview of the main themes of her life. It is impossible for us to go back in time and examine specific emotional episodes with any analytic rigor. We must settle for a review of her own and her biographers' accounts of the basic themes of her life and experience. Even such brief attention to the biographical setting of emotional experiences can, however, remind us of their slipperiness and variability from one context to another. And, importantly, it can alert us to the role that emotional experiences of wonder might play in fashioning a lifelong sensibility for what Carson called "the beauties and mysteries of the earth."[1]

Seeing Life's Beauties and Wonders

It is hard to imagine anyone less likely to mold national opinion than Rachel Carson (1907–64). A shy and soft-spoken woman, Rachel became the leading voice of the environmental movement that gained momentum in the 1960s. Her *Silent Spring* riveted national attention on the ecological dangers posed by the use of pesticides. The book sold more than half a million copies in hard cover and stayed on the *New York Times* best-seller list for thirty-one weeks. Though viciously attacked by business interests, *Silent Spring* succeeded in becoming what Stephen Fox has described as "one of the seminal volumes in conservation history: the *Uncle Tom's Cabin* of modern environmentalism."[2] Carson was personally battling cancer and other physical ailments as the book came under fire for its alarming claims concerning the health hazards created by widespread use of pesticides. Yet despite her personal infirmity, she courageously defended her cautionary message by making personal appearances in the media and testifying before governmental committees. Her plain yet eloquent

argument on behalf of our natural environment played a significant role in mobilizing public support for the regulation of human-made pollutants.

Rachel Carson grew up in a small town outside Pittsburgh, Pennsylvania. She later recalled that she was "rather a solitary child and spent a great deal of time in woods and beside streams, learning the birds and the insects and flowers."[3] Her family was poor. Rachel's father was never successful in the business world and never exerted much influence within the family, either. Rachel's mother, Marie Carson, was clearly the intellectual and emotional center of the family. Marie recognized her youngest child's promise and nurtured Rachel's appreciation for both nature and literature. Rachel would forever acknowledge that it was her mother who sparked in her a "love of life and of all living things." Because Rachel never married, the two lived together for the better part of Rachel's life. Marie's spiritual legacy to her daughter is captured in Rachel's recollection that "more than anyone else I know, she embodied Albert Schweitzer's 'reverence for life.'"[4]

On graduation from high school, Rachel entered Pennsylvania College for Women (now Chatham College) to major in English and become a writer. Midway through her junior year, however, she changed her major to zoology. At the time it appeared that Rachel was abandoning her literary aspirations. Rachel graduated from college with high honors and decided to pursue a master's degree in marine zoology at the Johns Hopkins University. There were few careers open to women in the 1930s—even those with graduate degrees. Rachel was fortunate to land a civil service position as a writer and editor with the Fish and Wildlife Services. One of the first two women ever to be hired by this governmental agency, Carson slowly worked her way up the bureaucratic ladder. She was initially hired as assistant aquatic biologist before being promoted to the positions of associate aquatic biologist, aquatic biologist, information specialist, and biologist and chief editor.

Carson worked diligently on an informational program on the sea for the Bureau of Fisheries. Her imagination as a creative writer

turned the piece into something more akin to poetry than governmental prose. Her supervisor was forced to tell her that the article was unacceptable for governmental use but that she might consider sending it to the *Atlantic*. She did. The finished work, titled "Undersea," was published in the *Atlantic Monthly* in 1937 and inaugurated a career that combined her interests in writing and marine biology. Simon and Schuster approached her after the article appeared in the *Atlantic* and signed her to a contract for her first book, *Under the Sea-Wind*. In 1951, Rachel published a second book, *The Sea around Us*. The book was a huge commercial success, staying near the top of the best-seller list for eighty-six weeks. The royalties from this book allowed her to resign from her governmental position and devote herself full-time to a life of disseminating the "reverence for life" she had acquired in childhood.

Carson was a careful, deliberate writer. She read her initial drafts out loud (often to her mother) before revising each sentence so that it conveyed not just information but a way of seeing the world. She would, for example, describe how "whenever I go down into this magical zone of the low water of the spring tides, I look for the most delicately beautiful of all the shore's inhabitants. . . . In that fairy cave I was not disappointed. . . . Here were creatures so exquisitely fashioned that they seemed unreal, their beauty too fragile to exist in a world of crushing force."[5] Her intention, of course, was to evoke the emotion of wonder in her readers. She sensed the tragedy in the fact that "most of us walk unseeing through the world, unaware alike of its beauties, its wonders, and the strange and sometimes terrible intensity of the lives that are being lived about us."[6]

Carson's ultimate objective in her writing was to evoke emotions that would cultivate an abiding reverence for life. It was not just the sea that she wrote about. It was a way of seeing the sea—a way that disrupts our shortsighted utilitarian frameworks and allows us, instead, to see how our entire existence connects with the cosmic flow of Life. To see the recurring patterns through which the sea has spawned life for thousands of years "is to have knowledge of things that are as nearly eternal as any earthly life can be. These things were

Rachel Carson (Photo taken by Shirley Briggs, ca. 1946; courtesy of the Lear/
Carson Collection, Connecticut College)

before ever humans stood on the shore of the ocean and looked out upon it with wonder; they continue year in, year out, through the centuries and the ages, while humanity's kingdoms rise and fall."[7] Viewing the world "in the long vistas of geologic time" altered Carson's vision in such a way as to grant the natural universe a value independent of human use. When seen against the cosmic background, "this same earth and sea have no need of us." Such vision reverses figure and ground, making human problems and motivations less relevant to the flow of life: "Perhaps if we reversed the telescope and looked at humans down these long vistas, we should find less time and inclination to plan for our own destruction."[8]

Cultivating a Reverence for Life

Rachel Carson, much like William James, arrived at what might be called an ethics of appreciation rather than an ethics of obedience to moral authority. Carson believed that moral conduct flows naturally from emotions producing empathy and identification. She observed that "in the artificial world of our cities and towns, we often forget the true nature of our planet and the long vistas of its history."[9] The unexpected beauty of nature, however, jars us out of everyday utilitarian rationality and elicits emotions that set us in search of meanings that somehow lie just beyond sensory appearances: "Underlying the beauty of the spectacle there is meaning and significance. It is the elusiveness of that meaning that haunts us, that sends us again and again into the natural world where the key to the riddle is hidden. It sends us back to the edge of the sea, where the . . . forces of evolution are at work today, as they have been since the appearance of what we know as life; and where the spectacle of living creatures faced by the cosmic realities of their world is crystal clear."[10]

Carson's lifelong mission was not simply to help others know about nature. It was to teach them how to feel about nature. As one of her biographers, Linda Lear, explains, "Wonder and awe were, for her, the highest emotions."[11] While outlining one of her major articles, Carson jotted down the basic creed that guided her personal and

professional life: "Once you are *aware* of the wonder and beauty of earth, you will want to learn about it." The article went on to elaborate how the emotion of wonder produces a proper reverence for life: "Once the emotions have been aroused—a sense of the beautiful, the excitement of the new and the unknown, a feeling of sympathy, pity, admiration or love—then we wish for knowledge about the object of our emotional response. Once found, it has lasting meaning."[12] Carson placed her final hope for the survival of life on the empathy, compassion, and care aroused by the emotion of wonder. "I believe," she wrote, "that the more clearly we can focus our attention on the wonders and realities of the universe about us, the less taste we shall have for destruction."[13]

What Rachel Carson teaches us is that wonder is a profoundly functional emotion. This is in sharp contrast to the position taken by many evolutionary theorists such as Richard Dawkins, Scott Atran, and Steven Pinker. Dawkins, for example, acknowledges humanity's "appetite for wonder" but insists that this appetite is something that only "real science ought to be feeding" or it will lead only to delusion. Atran and Pinker, we might recall, believe that wonder is an example of the application of mental tools to problems other than those the mind was designed by natural selection to solve. Carson saw the matter quite differently. She acknowledged that humanity's technological rationality is sufficiently developed so that we are now capable of taking over many of the functions of God. Yet, she cautioned, "as humans approach the 'new heaven and the new earth'—or the space-age universe . . . they must do so with humility rather than arrogance." To this she added, "And along with humility I think there is still a place for wonder."[14]

Carson placed humility and wonder at the core of her spiritual orientation to life. She told a group of journalists that the emotions aroused by natural beauty have "a necessary place in the spiritual development of any individual or any society. I believe that whenever we substitute something human-made and artificial for a natural feature of the earth, we have retarded some part of humanity's spiritual growth."[15] Carson was a deeply spiritual person. Yet she believed

that genuine spirituality emerged from wonder at the facts of nature, not from submitting our minds to ancient scriptures. Thus humility, wonder, and a reverence for life—not adherence to institutional religion—were for her the spiritual virtues suited to the ongoing flow of life.[16]

Rachel found herself in midlife suddenly faced with responsibility of caring for the future. When her niece passed away, Rachel assumed the task of raising her grandnephew, Roger. It was while reflecting on how best to raise Roger that Rachel penned an article for *Woman's Home Companion* entitled "Help Your Child to Wonder." This article, later published with photographic illustrations as *A Sense of Wonder*, captured Carson's maturing vision of how we might help a new generation develop a reverence for life. She began this discourse by noting that "a child's world is fresh and new and beautiful, full of wonder and excitement. It is our misfortune that for most of us that clear-eyed vision, that true instinct for what is beautiful and awe-inspiring, is dimmed and even lost before we reach adulthood." She then ventured, "If I had influence with the good fairy who is supposed to preside over the christening of all children I should ask that her gift to each child in the world be a sense of wonder so indestructible that it would last throughout life, as an unfailing antidote against the boredom and disenchantments of later years, the sterile preoccupation with things that are artificial, the alienation from the sources of our strength."[17]

Carson understood well the kinds of skepticism that a Dawkins, Atran, or Pinker might have about the importance of the emotion of wonder. Wonder is surely not linked with early humanity's hunting and gathering survival tasks. She was quite aware that wonder sets us in search of meanings and truths that lie just beyond the boundaries of human existence. Yet this is precisely why she believed wonder to be a virtue necessary for the long-term survival of our species.

What is the value of preserving and strengthening this sense of awe and wonder, this recognition of something beyond the boundaries of human existence? Is the exploration of the natural

world just a pleasant way to pass the golden hours of childhood or is there something deeper?

I am sure there is something much deeper, something lasting and significant. Those who dwell, as scientists or laymen, among the beauties and mysteries of the earth are never alone or weary of life. . . . Their thoughts can find paths that lead to inner contentment and to renewed excitement in living. Those who contemplate the beauty of the earth find reserves of strength that will endure as long as life lasts.[18]

Carson did not expect wonder to lead to the same kinds of truth that we expect from science or logical analysis. As she wrote elsewhere, wonder instead awakens a passion for "some universal truth that lies just beyond our grasp . . . [a meaning that] haunts and ever eludes us, and in its very pursuit we approach the ultimate mystery of Life itself."[19] It is this kind of truth, a truth that is noetic and transient, that leads to renewed excitement in living and unlocks reserves of strength with which we might care for life around us. The ongoing pursuit of a truth "just beyond our grasp" engages us in life; it draws us out into sustained activity on behalf of the larger world. It is, in Carson's view, the sense of wonder that best elicits and sustains a reverence for life. Her cautionary message was that a life without wonder puts humanity's long-term future in jeopardy.

8. Experience and Personal Transformation

The most beautiful thing we can experience is the
mysterious. It is the source of all true art and all science.
He to whom this emotion is a stranger, who can no
longer pause to wonder and stand rapt in awe, is as good
as dead; his eyes are closed.—ALBERT EINSTEIN

ACHEL CARSON DREW ATTENTION TO THE FACT THAT
wonder seems to arise quite frequently in children. So much
in life strikes children as novel or as intensely powerful. Adults, however, have fewer direct or unmediated experiences.
Adults filter, sort, and label experience through fairly stable cognitive
categories. Their experience of the world thus tends to elicit less emotional reaction than children's experience. This undoubtedly explains why certain novel or unexpected experiences—if they overflow
the perceptual and cognitive categories that would ordinarily constrain them—have such a profound effect on adults. Such wonder-
filled experiences have the subjective sense of being fresh, direct, and
unmediated. They hint at disclosing information from which we are
ordinarily cut off. They consequently transform the way we perceive
and think about the world.

Any number of experiences might elicit wonder and give rise to

significant personal transformation. William James, for example, had his entire sensibility for what is "real" transformed by the altered state of consciousness induced by nitrous oxide. The experience, he wrote, was a "tremendously exciting sense of an intense metaphysical illumination." His experiences with spiritualism and other occult activities also emboldened him to abandon strictly scientific understandings and to embrace a range of metaphysical beliefs. We might further illustrate how certain unexpected experiences transform our perceptual and cognitive sensibilities by selecting four additional examples of wonder-filled human activity: deep encounters with others; aesthetic response to the fine or performing arts; scientific discovery; and the practice of meditation or other mystical disciplines. All four are valued by humans for providing experiences that Einstein described as helping us "pause to wonder and stand rapt in awe."

Encountering Others

The writings of the Jewish philosopher Martin Buber provide eloquent depictions of the wondrous possibilities of human relationships. Buber acknowledged that we spend the bulk of our lives regarding others as "objects" of our experience. Others appear to us only as means to our own ends. Buber referred to this fundamental structure of human experience as the I-It relationship. Yet, Buber notes, on rare occasions we enter into forms of relationships that cause us to acknowledge the independent existence and intrinsic worth of another person. Such relationships are truly dialogical. They help us beyond our usual egocentric orientation to the world, radically redefining both I-ness and otherness.

Buber maintained that such dialogical relationships disclose the deepest meanings of human existence. In his words, "All real living is meeting."[1] The dialogical, according to Buber, is its own unique sphere of human existence. Buber wanted to make it clear that he was identifying something that has an ontological status over and beyond subjective feeling. He therefore referred to this separate sphere of experience as "between." His point is that some encounters between

people take place outside the subject-object (I-It) sphere of existence. Buber explains that life is full of "fleeting, yet consistent happenings" that take us beyond the realm of I-It relationships to a genuinely dialogical mode of being. The category of "between" was for him "the real place and bearer of what happens between persons." That is, whenever we encounter others not through dull habit but instead in a genuine meeting, "what is essential *does not take place in* each of the participants *but takes places between* them in the most precise sense, as it were in a dimension which is accessible only to them both."[2]

Buber observed that whenever he had personally opened up to this sphere of betweenness, "something happens to me."[3] Unexpected encounters with the very being of another person confront us as a limit to our initial egocentrism. They draw us out to a new world of relatedness outside the world of I-It relationships. And, importantly, they make it possible for us to realize that the other person is no longer an "it" but a "thou." Entering the world of "I-Thou" relationships is life-transforming. The "thou" appears to us as an expression of the creative power of life itself. In Buber's words, "Every particular Thou is a glimpse through to the eternal Thou."[4]

Buber believed that the transformative power of truly dialogical relationships implies something about the cosmos itself. I-Thou encounters invite reflection on the presence of the sacred in our lives.[5] Buber contended that genuine human encounters disclose the presence of a sacred power capable of hallowing life. Buber was in this way being faithful to the Jewish prophetic tradition. Prophetic witness calls on us to encounter God not in the temple but in our encounters with others. For Buber, then, the only real way to encounter the eternal "Thou" is to encounter the particular "thou" of another person. Every human relationship is potentially a portal to the eternal "Thou." In Buber's words, "every particular Thou is a glimpse through to the eternal Thou." Buber thus thought of spirituality not as devotion to a transcendent being but as our response to the "thou" of another person. It follows, then, that genuine religious faith is not about believing in ancient Bible stories but instead about a very particular way of seeing: "A great genuine history-faith does not

come into the world through interpretation of the extra-historical as historical, but by receiving an occurrence experienced as a 'wonder,' that is an event which cannot be grasped except as an act of God."[6]

According to Buber, spirituality is to be found though genuine relatedness to others. He explained that such spirituality requires an acquired ability to "receive an experience as a wonder." Buber observed that we are filled with wonder whenever we see an event not only as existing within the causal nexus known to science but also as a meeting with God. Buber acknowledged that both the philosopher (rationalist) and the religious person wonder at unexpected phenomena. But, says Buber, while the philosopher neutralizes wonder in abstract theory, the religious person "abides in that wonder."[7] A life shaped by I-Thou encounters is a life that more fully abides in wonder.

The psychologist Carl Rogers also wrote extensively about the transformative potential of interpersonal relationships. Rogers began his career in psychotherapy at a time when the therapist was thought to be the center of the therapeutic enterprise. The therapist, after all, brings a great deal of experience and theoretical knowledge to the counseling relationship. Rogers, however, came to believe that every person possesses within him- or herself the resources for self-integration and growth. What he called "client-centered" therapy required only that the therapist provide a safe emotional environment within which clients might let go of their defenses and get in touch with their own inner resources.

Rogers's therapeutic approach met with great success. He found that the majority of his clients needed little more than to be understood. Few of them had ever received warmth or empathy from others. Rogers used therapy to redress this situation, providing a warm, accepting environment in which his clients could be free to explore their thoughts and feelings. He believed that the therapist's main objective should be to offer clients "unconditional positive regard"; that is, the therapist should show genuine empathy and accept the client for who she or he is rather than imposing moral judgments.

Rogers found that to the degree that therapists were able to pro-

vide this unconditional positive regard, clients were able to open up to the full range of their own inner experience and would begin moving in the direction of personal growth and wholeness. The experience of being understood and accepted proved to be both a necessary and sufficient cause of significant personal growth. His clients routinely reported that they had gained a greater trust in their own emotional reactions, a feeling of being in control of their own lives rather than being controlled by others, and a new vitality that comes from living fully in the moment.

Rogers found that entering into warm, empathic relationships with others had a profound effect on him, too. He observed, "It is a sparkling thing when I encounter realness in another person."[8] What struck Rogers most about these intimate encounters was his discovery that the thoughts and feelings we have always thought are deeply personal and unique to ourselves are actually quite common. As he put it, "What is most personal is most general."[9] Empathic relationships disclose levels of personal experience that seem to go beyond the individual. That is, the deepest levels of experience seem to attest to the presence and causal activity of something "more." Rogers explained that "there is another peculiar satisfaction in really hearing someone: It is like listening to the music of the spheres, because beyond the immediate message of the person, no matter what that might be, there is the universal."[10]

Rogers's point is that truly hearing another person creates the sensation that one is simultaneously in the presence of something more than physical. Rogers wrote, "When I can really hear someone, it puts me in touch with him; it enriches my life. . . . So there is both the satisfaction of hearing this person and also the satisfaction of feeling one's self in touch with what is universally true."[11] And, according to Rogers, such wondrous encounters with others occasioned profound personal growth in him as well. "In my own two-way communication with others there have been experiences that have made me feel pleased and warm and good and satisfied. . . . [These experiences] have made me feel expanded, larger, enriched, and have accelerated my own growth."[12]

Thus Rogers, like Buber, came to believe that certain modes of human relationship trigger unexpected experiences. They dismantle our subject-object orientation to life and foster belief in the existence of some deeper kind of reality that is not "out there" in any straightforward way. Such experiences are, moreover, both profound and transforming. Buber observed that "without It a human being cannot live. But whoever lives only with that is not human."[13] The practical demands of daily existence require us to orient ourselves to life viewing others as the objects of our experience. Without this utilitarian viewpoint we cannot live. But we are not fully human if we do not also enter into relationships that help us—at least momentarily— "abide in wonder." Sure, we can go through life without wonder-filled relationships with others. But to do so would be to live without the kinds of growth and transformation that make human life intrinsically significant.

Fine and Performing Arts

The psychologist Howard Gardner has written extensively on the topic of human intelligence. Gardner is convinced that humans possess a wide variety of mental abilities and that each should be considered its own unique form of intelligence. He has proposed, for example, that we recognize the existence of such diverse forms of intelligence as spatial intelligence, bodily kinesthetic intelligence, and linguistic intelligence. Gardner has even suggested that humans possess a discrete form of intelligence that he terms "spiritual intelligence." He defines spiritual intelligence in terms of our varying capacities to engage "cosmic issues": Who are we? Where do we come from? Why do we exist? What is the meaning of love, of life, of death? Spiritual intelligence is thus "the capacity to locate oneself with respect to the furthest reaches of the cosmos."[14]

Gardner confesses that he is not personally religious. He acknowledges, however, that certain aesthetic experiences prompt him to contemplate a range of cosmic issues. He is susceptible to the spiritual qualities of certain kinds of music. Especially intricate music

arrests his active will and causes him to contemplate a more general order of existence from which such beauty must flow. He writes, "I lose track of mundane concerns, alter my perception of space and time, and, occasionally, feel in touch with issues of cosmic import."[15] Such experiences cause him to feel that he has been enriched, ennobled, and humbled. Gardner thus draws our attention to the fact that aesthetic experiences often evoke the emotion of wonder (and the transformation of perception and cognition that the experience of wonder typically induces).

The connection between wonder and the arts was introduced in the first chapter of this book in a discussion of the canonical Indian text known as the *Natyashastra*. Some of the most interesting recent studies in human emotion have, in fact, been conducted by humanities scholars in various fields of Asian history and religion.[16] This is especially true in regard to scholarship dealing with the *Natyashastra*, which investigates the nature of consciousness (particularly the effect that drama and other aesthetic experiences have in producing insight or revelatory changes in consciousness).[17] This text attempts to categorize the various emotional responses engendered by theater and literature. The purpose was to understand how such art forms might invoke these emotional responses and elicit an experience of Brahman (the ultimate power of the universe that is immanent in all of existence). The sixth chapter of the *Natyashastra* distills centuries of thought on this topic by enumerating the nine basic emotions: sexual passion, amusement, sorrow, anger, fear, perseverance, disgust, serenity, and wonder. The Indian notion of wonder means something more than just being surprised or startled by the sudden perception of some unexpected event. The *Natyashastra* describes wonder as a reaction to a perception of divine, heavenly, or exalted phenomena. Hindu theology maintains that God, or absolute consciousness, is immanent in all things. For this reason, the act of "seeing" the divine is believed to result from aesthetic experiences that momentarily enable us to bridge the usual gap between subject and object. Temple icons, plays, or even particularly beautiful scenes in nature are thought to be capable of enabling people to feel as though

they are actually participating in the very essence of the object they perceive (including participating in the divine ground of this object). Classical Hindu thought thus argues that aesthetic experiences—by eliciting wonder—can potentially take a person beyond his or her own individuality to participate in a greater ontological whole.

There are probably no Western texts that so thoroughly examine the relationship between the arts and emotion as the *Natyashastra*. Yet the connections between aesthetic experience, emotions, and spirituality have received at least some philosophical and psychological attention. The psychologist Robert Kegan, for example, describes how certain works of art have prompted him to consider "how alive they seemed, how they traveled beyond their canvas to something somehow true, whether natural or abstract."[18] Kegan's personal observation confirms what we have already learned about how experiences of wonder affect our perceptual and cognitive processes. He recounts that works of art evoke a feeling of intense vitality and direct his attention to "travel beyond" the particular object of sensation and seek the causal source of its beauty, life, or power at a more general order of existence. Works of art, in other words, often incite an experience of wonder.

It is interesting to speculate on just why the fine and performing arts so often succeed in stimulating wonder. One of most widely acclaimed researchers in the field of emotions, Keith Oatley, believes that the visual arts explore the basic tension between assimilation and accommodation as adaptive modalities. Oatley maintains that emotions arise when we consciously or unconsciously evaluate an event as related to our needs or interests.[19] Our natural tendency when viewing visual art is to assimilate its patterns and forms to our existing cognitive schemata. This perceptual activity inherently produces arousal and pleasure.[20] Some works of art, however, are not easily assimilated to existing schemata. They prompt us to learn, to accommodate to new perceptual and cognitive schemata. This experience of accommodation (possibly owing to the combination of wonder, interest, and joy that Izard connects with the ability to engage the environment freely and creatively) is itself often pleasurable.

In fact, research has shown "we are drawn to what is too complex for our understanding, and also to mystery, the seeming invitation to what may lie just round the corner."[21] Oatley conjectures that "assimilation and accommodation, derived respectively from the schematically attractive and the not-yet-understood, are always in tension. Art, with its basis of schema plus elaboration, is often the exploration of such tension."[22]

Music, like abstract visual art, also affects the human nervous system without relying on human words or gestures. Just how and why music comes to have meaning for listeners is at heart a philosophical question. Composers, performers, and aestheticians tend to divide into one of two major theoretical camps concerning music's role in arousing emotional response.[23] The first theoretical camp consists of "absolutists," who argue that musical meaning lies exclusively within the context of the work itself. The second theoretical camp consists of "referentialists," who contend that, in addition to its inherent meanings, music communicates meanings that in some way refer to concepts, memories, or emotional states that exist independent of the music itself.

Common sense finally causes us to side with the referentialists. Listeners' memories, cultural background, and previous musical experiences all affect their emotional response to a work of music. But this should not divert us from also appreciating the way that music actively structures stimulus situations and thereby makes some emotional responses more likely than others. Indeed, there has been considerable research in the field of "music and the emotions," and there is compelling evidence in support of the view that people discern very similar emotional expression while listening to the same piece of music.[24] Emotions arise in the face of unexpected or uncertain stimuli. Discrepancies between past expectations and seemingly anomalous new stimuli create uncertainty. This uncertainty activates the brain's emotion programs designed to mobilize the organism for appropriate response. This, it seems, is precisely how musical compositions evoke emotions in us—including the emotion of wonder.

Rhythm, melody, and harmonic order structure time and there-

fore make it possible for listeners to anticipate a certain kind of predictable order.[25] Music, then, creates a sensory universe. By controlling the flow of stimuli to the mind, music structures experiences of ambiguity, uncertainty, and suspense. Musical compositions typically set a norm, deviate from that norm, then return to it. In this way music creates expectations in the listener. Emotions—both in "real life" and when viewing the fine or performing arts—result when experience diverges significantly from our expectations. When experience falls short of anticipation (or promises to impede our satisfaction of vital needs or interests), we have "negative" emotions. Thus, for example, if a friend or loved one fails to show up for a long-awaited meeting, we feel sad. Yet when experience exceeds anticipation (or promises to satisfy our needs and interests), we have "positive" emotions. Such would be the case if our favorite sports team upsets a heavily favored opponent. In just this way musical compositions can create norms or expectations and then deviate from them in ways that generate fairly predictable emotional responses.

Listening to music typically creates a carefully ordered experience. As Robert Jourdain comments in *Music, the Brain, and Ecstasy*, "In daily life, a brain does its best to make sense of a disorderly world. It easily finds the most superficial relations among the objects it encounters. But a brain doesn't often encounter immaculate deep relations in the world around it, for the simple reason that there are few that are readily perceived."[26] Music provides experiences of order in ways that daily life can rarely match. Consider, for example, how the many component sections of an orchestra—each of which initially operates independently—come together to resolve ambiguity and conclude in perfect harmony. Jourdain notes that "the experience of unsullied order persisting simultaneously at every perceptual level may be taken as a working definition of the word 'beauty.' . . . By providing the brain with an artificial environment, and forcing it through that environment in controlled ways, music imparts the means of experiencing relations far deeper than we encounter in our everyday lives."[27]

Music, then, has a unique ability to structure wonder-ful experi-

ence. It structures "surprise discoveries" of beauty. It enables us to discern a deeper order lurking just beneath the surface of sensory patterns. Catching a glimpse of this "deeper order" is in itself an experience of ecstasy; that is, it allows us to feel that, however briefly, we have attained a greater grasp of the world and its possibilities. Music consequently makes the world appear more orderly than it is from a strictly rational perspective. It offers us the opportunity to respond to intense displays of beauty and order and in so doing to be transformed by the expansive emotion of wonder. The emotional response evoked by music, according to Jourdain, is not just a response "to the beauty of the sustained deep relations that are revealed, but also to the fact of our perceiving them. As our brains are thrown into overdrive, we feel our very existence expand and realize that we can be more than we normally are, and the world is more than it seems. This is cause enough for ecstasy."[28]

All aesthetic experiences are not so ecstatic. Nor do all evoke an act of religious "seeing," which the *Natyashastra* extols as one of art's principal goals. But many aesthetic experiences do evoke the wondrous sense that we have discerned the presence and causal activity of a higher order of things. This is why Bernice and Richard Lazarus argue that aesthetic experiences arouse what they call "the empathic emotions." They observe that most people react emotionally to theater, paintings, music, and the sights and sounds of natural scenes such as sunsets and the evening sky. The Lazaruses find that such experiences frequently evoke "awe or wonder, which can be likened to religious experience."[29] They go on to note that "awe may involve dread or have the positive connotation of wonder and joy over discoveries about the world, its vastness, or the remarkable gifts of life and intelligence. These states, which certainly seem to be emotional, may be blends of other emotions. The words for them also have spiritual connotations."[30] To this extent contemporary Western social scientists seem to echo the view held by ancient Indian sages that aesthetic experiences are a vehicle that can momentarily make us "see" how our lives participate in some greater ontological whole.

Mathematics and music have a great deal in common. Both mathematicians and musicians create patterns. These patterns bring order out of chaos and bring otherwise disconnected entities into relationship. Furthermore, mathematics—no less than music—evokes aesthetic experiences. One of the most important criteria by which musical or mathematical patterns are judged is whether they occasion the human perception of beauty. The highly regarded British mathematician G. H. Hardy remarked, "A mathematician, like a painter or a poet, is a maker of patterns. . . . The mathematician's patterns, like the painter's or the poet's, must be beautiful, the ideas, like the colours or the words, must fit together in a harmonious way. Beauty is the first test: there is no permanent place in the world for ugly mathematics."[31]

The French mathematician Henri Poincaré also discerned an aesthetic element in the personal drive to investigate mathematical patterns. He observed that mathematicians "study mathematics because they delight in it and they delight in it because it is beautiful."[32] According to Poincaré, the human mind finds it intrinsically rewarding to come across instances of "harmony beautiful to contemplate." Theoretical mathematics leads to unexpected moments of beauty. It is for this reason that mathematicians commonly concede that no one "can be a complete mathematician unless they are also something of a poet."[33] Poetry, of course, achieves its emotional response through the element of surprise. Poets bring otherwise disparate human experiences into juxtaposition, leading the reader to discover unexpected patterns of meaning that connect with their own lives. John Keats put this succinctly when he noted that "poetry should surprise . . . it should strike readers as a wording of their own highest thoughts, and appear almost a remembrance."[34] Like poetry, mathematical inquiry also leads to surprise at discerning unexpected meanings and order. This is undoubtedly why so many people are engaged by mathematics, finding that it draws them forward in the pursuit of beauty and order.

The most commonly cited example of how mathematics can unleash the emotion of wonder is the mystery surrounding the number Phi. One way of deriving the numerical value of Phi is from the Fibonacci sequence (i.e., the sequence that derives each new term from the sum of the two previous terms—1, 2, 3, 5, 8, 13, and so on). If we examine the ratios of each successive pair of numbers, we come upon a sequence approaching Phi (1.618 . . .). What is so astonishing about this number is that it spontaneously appears in the most unexpected places. If we count the female bees in a beehive and divide that number by the total of male bees, we approach the number Phi. Or if we examine the ratio of successive spirals on a mollusk, we again arrive at Phi. The ratio of successive rows of seeds in a sunflower similarly equals Phi. And if we calculate the ratio of line segments in a pentacle, all these ratios will equal Phi. Nor does it end there. Instances of Phi appear throughout the world in great works of architecture (e.g., the Great Pyramid) as well as great music compositions (e.g., Beethoven's Fifth Symphony). Not only does the ubiquity of Phi in nature exceed coincidence, but phenomena that express this number also seem to have an especially pleasing or beautiful appeal to the human mind. For these reasons the number Phi has for centuries been designated with such honorific titles as the "Divine Proportion," the "Golden Number," or the "Golden Ratio."

The number Phi illustrates the interplay between order and surprise in mathematical inquiry. It also exemplifies the power of mathematics to elicit wonder. The sudden appearance of Phi where least expected constitutes a vivid experience of "a perception of something novel and unexpected" and "astonishment mingled with perplexity or bewildered curiosity." It is thus only to be expected that the surprise discovery of Phi triggers the emotion of wonder. In his book *The Divine Proportion: A Study in Mathematical Beauty*, H. E. Huntley comments that "the sense of surprise" that arises when we stumble across unexpected appearances of the number Phi in nature "appears to be compounded of a mixture of archaic emotions." Such surprise, he observes, gives rise to a mixture of the archaic emotions of curiosity and wonder. While curiosity motivates us to find a more

detailed understanding of the "specifics" we have encountered, wonder leads to speculation and anticipation concerning the existence of as yet undiscovered worlds.

> There is *surprise* at the unexpected encounter; there is also both curiosity and wonder—making three of the flavors included in the idea of beauty. *Curiosity*: because one craves to understand why Phi, which permeates the pentagram and is at home in Platonic polyhedra, should also be the limit of a ratio initiated so casually. . . . *Wonder*: because the conviction grows stronger that we have chanced on an unexplored world which, like the universe around us, appears to have no boundaries. There must, we speculate, be other discoveries to be made here by the inquiring mind.[35]

Unexpected appearances of Phi alert the mind to search for the agency responsible for such vivid instances of beauty and order. They unleash wonder and thus stir up "strong convictions" in the possible presence of unexplored worlds teeming with as yet unexplored possibility. It is easy to see why mathematical discovery so often seems to have a Platonic flair. Plato, who believed that our phenomenal world is but a shadowy reflection of a transcendent realm of pure order and beauty, once commented that "the knowledge at which geometry aims is the knowledge of the eternal."[36] Most mathematicians today would concede that Platonism is no longer tenable as a philosophical framework for mathematical theory and would instead emphasize the role of the human mind in constructing (as opposed to simply discovering) mathematical knowledge. Yet there is a common joke among mathematicians that they are "constructivists" during the official workweek but go home and pursue their mathematical investigations as closet Platonists over the weekend. After all, "divine numbers" do appear throughout nature. While most mathematical structures are contrived inventions of the human mind, some seem to be discoveries in which the mathematician stumbles upon universal patterns that appear to be anchored in reality outside the human mind. The British physicist and mathematician Roger Penrose summarized this dilemma when he asked:

Is mathematics invention or discovery? When mathematicians come upon their results are they just producing elaborate mental constructions which have no actual reality, but whose power and elegance is sufficient simply to fool even their inventors into believing that these mental constructions are "real"? Or, are mathematicians really uncovering truths which are, in fact, already "there"—truths whose existence is quite independent of the mathematicians' activities? I think that, by now, it must be clear to the reader that I am an adherent of the second, rather than the first, view.[37]

Penrose is thus one for whom mathematical experience gives rise to wonder. It sets loose in him what Huntley described as the quest for "an unexplored world" that might account for such otherwise unanticipated instances of beauty and order. The sense of surprise underlying mathematical discoveries might only occasion curiosity in some people. But in others it evokes a strong sense of wonder. It generates feelings of awe and fascination and prompts us to speculate about the presence and causal relevance of a metaphysical order of things.

Surprise, curiosity, and wonder are also emotions that frequently arise in scientific inquiry. This is true even though science has for at least three hundred years sought to identify itself exclusively with surprise and curiosity, hoping to rid itself of the metaphysical speculation to which wonder often leads. Aristotle was among the first to clarify the nature of scientific inquiry and to eliminate the mystical or intuitive methods of his mentor, Plato. Unlike Plato, Aristotle believed that knowledge comes to us through our senses (rather than through intuitive reason). Aristotle was thereby paving the way for scientific inquiry grounded squarely in empirical data that can be publicly verified and quantitatively analyzed. Aristotle also sharpened the scientific enterprise by carefully distinguishing between different understandings of what constitutes a cause. Events can be explained with reference to any one of four different conceptions of a cause: the material cause (the substance of which something is

made); the formal cause (the form of something or class to which it belongs); the efficient cause (the direct impetus of change); and the final cause (the intention, purpose, goal of an action. Over the centuries science has largely distinguished itself from philosophy and theology by concentrating on the efficient (and, to a lesser extent, the material) cause of an event. Science has eschewed discussions of final causes (i.e., attempting to discern the meaning, purpose, or intentionality of events) as insusceptible to public verification or quantitative analysis—and hence inconsistent with the scientific goal of yielding precise knowledge about the world.

The elimination of "final cause" explanations from scientific inquiry greatly affected the emotional triad of surprise-curiosity-wonder. The "surprise" engendered through scientific investigation has ever since been channeled solely into curiosity. That is, scientific surprise is supposed to set us in search of the specific material or efficient causes that produced unexpected data. Scientific curiosity is inherently reductive. Its goal is to isolate the smallest possible units that constitute the material or efficient causes responsible for observed phenomena. Wonder, on the other hand, directs us to speculate not about the particulars of an unexpected event but about its relationship to a greater whole. It is therefore no longer an emotion consistent with the scientific enterprise per se. Aristotle's early distinctions about causation thus eventually gave rise to a form of scientific inquiry that enshrines curiosity as the emotion par excellence while linking wonder with superstition or intellectual backwardness.

The scientific method's inadvertent tendency to extol the emotion of curiosity at the expense of wonder is in many ways at variance with humanity's intellectual and existential concerns. Humans are engaged in two distinct kinds of search concerning the world in which we live. First, we are engaged in a search for intelligibility. We wish to understand the workings of our world as reliably as possible. Science—including its quest to reduce phenomena to the language of material and efficient causation—embodies this quest for intelligibility. The principal (though not exclusive) way that science has rendered the universe more intelligible is by amplifying our emotion of

curiosity and devising methods to break down complex phenomena into smaller, more readily analyzed units.

We are also, however, engaged in a quest for personal meaning. We desire to understand the meaning of existence in general and our own existence in particular. Such understanding comes by pushing "why" questions in the opposite direction ordinarily pursued in scientific investigation. Questions of meaning have to do with how individual phenomena or parts relate to a larger whole. This, of course, is the direction of thought motivated by the emotion of wonder. Chapter 6 examined how the emotion of wonder motivates cognitive operations that construct larger contexts for answering the "why" questions that emerge in human experience. Wonder enables us to perform the vital cognitive functions that Piaget described as the ability to think "beyond the present and form theories about everything, delighting especially in considerations of that which is not [present to the senses]." Wonder enhances our ability to think hypothetically, to construct models of what might possibly account for unexpected phenomena or especially vivid instances of beauty, order, and vitality. Wonder thus plays a critical role in our efforts to accommodate to the ever greater orders of life. It does so, however, by generating constructions of what is possible. The difficulty of wonder-born thought is that we lack any means of empirically testing most of these conceptions of what is possible. Wonder-born thought, precisely because it engages issues of what might be the "final" or "ultimate" cause of life, lacks the kind of intelligibility of causal explanations restricted to material- and efficient-cause explanations.

Most scientists are aware that both curiosity and wonder fuel their scientific investigations, even if they must finally suspend their sense of wonder at the point they press for the intelligibility of efficient-cause explanations of observed phenomena. The psychologist Robert Plutchik, for example, featured a quotation on the frontispiece of *Emotions and Life* that summarizes what he deems to be the heart of scientific investigation: "Science starts with fascination and wonder."[38] In a similar vein, the highly regarded evolutionary theorist Ernst Mayr wrote that "virtually all biologists are religious, in the

deeper sense of this word, even though it may be a religion without revelation. . . . The unknown and maybe unknowable instills in us a sense of humility and awe."[39] Mayr's point would appear to be that wonder ("a sense of humility and awe") is the root source of our fundamental drive to understand the nature and meaning of the universe. Scientists are motivated by both curiosity and wonder, even if the element of wonder is methodologically muted in their formal pronouncements. It was with this point in mind that the evolutionary theorist Arthur Peacocke commented that "the scientifically reductionist account has a limited range and needs to be incorporated into a larger theistic framework that has been constructed in response to questions of the kind, Why is there anything at all? And What kind of universe must it be if insentient matter can evolve naturally into self-conscious, thinking persons? And What is the meaning of personal life in such a cosmos?"[40]

Science, as science, is not expected to seek accommodation to larger frameworks that seek to answer such questions. These are questions that invariably encourage consideration of the possible role that final (i.e., owing to purpose, goal direction, or intention) or ultimate (i.e., owing to the agency of some extramundane order of things) causes play in our universe. As such, they are not properly scientific. Nonetheless, scientific considerations of causality—taken to their limit—invite us to incorporate them into precisely such higher-order interpretive frameworks. And scientists—who are surprised by the beauty, order, and vitality of this universe on a daily basis—are precisely those most susceptible to the awe and wonder that motivate such efforts at accommodation to a higher or larger order of things.

Science, as an institution of modern culture, pursues reliable knowledge about nature by seeking to reduce natural phenomena to their material and efficient causes. But scientists themselves often delight in seeking patterns and design that evoke wonder concerning the possible ultimate causes that might lie behind these patterns. The cell biologist Ursula Goodenough has confessed that the scientific aim of restricting notions of causality to efficient causes not only robs

the universe of meaning but also fosters a sense of nihilism that she finds personally deflating. She writes,

> I have come to understand that I can deflect the apparent pointlessness of it all by realizing that I don't have to seek a point. In any of it. Instead, I can see [natural phenomena] as the locus of Mystery.
>
> – The Mystery of why there is anything at all, rather than nothing.
> – The Mystery of where the laws of physics came from.
> – The Mystery of why the universe seems so strange.[41]

Goodenough's contemplation of what she calls "the sacred depth of nature" leads her to affirm a religious naturalism. By this she means that it is possible to affirm simultaneously both the lawfulness of nature and its embodiment of a fundamental mystery. Her spiritual impulse doesn't quest for information or factual propositions that somehow prove science false. Instead, she quests for a spirituality informed by science but animated by wonder: "To be sure the *beauty of nature*—sunsets, woodlands, fireflies—has *elicited religious emotions* throughout the ages. We are moved to awe and *wonder* at the grandeur, the poetry, the richness of natural beauty; it fills us with joy and thanksgiving."[42]

Goodenough believes that the mystery inherent in the very existence of the natural universe "generates wonder, and wonder generates awe." She has found that these emotions are sufficient to transform the scientific account of nature into a spiritually charged cosmology. That is, it is important to her that her personal outlook on life be grounded in scientifically accepted understandings of how things are. Science is, however, to her a necessary but not sufficient basis for the kind of "planetary ethic" capable of sustaining humanity in the twenty-first century. Only when science yields to the emotions of wonder and awe can it finally instill "a reverence for how life works, and acknowledge a deep and complex imperative that life continue."[43]

In *Experience and God*, theologian John E. Smith defined religion as the quest to go beyond profane existence. Humans, he contends, have an enduring desire to experience, even if only momentarily, an utterly different order of existence that is best termed the *sacred* or the *holy*. By profane existence Smith meant the taken-for-granted aspects of everyday life. Profane existence is ordinary. Because it is ordinary, it fails to evoke consideration of the more-than-ordinary that might reveal to us the meaning or purpose of life. Smith explains that "the daily round of events is ordinary enough and gives *no occasion for wonder* or special concern. In the ordinary events there is no question of judgment on life as a whole. . . . [They] harbor no mystery, nor call forth the sense that beyond and beneath our life is a holy ground."[44]

It is, Smith argues, experiences that "give occasion for wonder" that signal the first glimpse of the sacred. Wonder-filled experiences take us beyond ordinary events to consider judgments on life as a whole. They harbor mystery, calling forth a sense of what is beyond or beneath ordinary experience. The psychoanalyst and social philosopher Erich Fromm made a very similar point when he observed that

> one aspect of religious experience is the *wondering*, the marveling, the becoming aware of life and of one's own existence, and of the puzzling problem of one's relatedness to the world. . . . Socrates' statement that *wonder is the beginning of* all wisdom is true not only for wisdom but for the *religious experience*. One who has never been bewildered, who has never looked upon life and his own existence as phenomena which require answers and yet, paradoxically, for which the only answers are new questions, can hardly understand what religious experience is.[45]

The religious quest is thus part and parcel of experiences that "occasion wonder." The spiritual path begins with wonder. That is, the quest for the sacred requires changes in our perceptual and cog-

nitive orientations to life. It requires that we become alert to the possible presence and causal relevance of a more general order of things. It is for this reason that every religious tradition has included some normative role for spiritual practices whose goal is to occasion precisely such wonder-driven changes in perception and cognition. These spiritual practices are variously referred to as contemplative exercises, mystical disciplines, or meditation. Their aim is to help us move past the profane or ordinary world to experiences that give occasion for wonder. Spiritual practices accomplish this by devising mental exercises that eventually free us from all conditioning and habitual mental functions. As Piaget and other cognitive psychologists have demonstrated, the course of psychological development from birth through adolescence consists of the gradual acquisition of cognitive structures that enable us to interpret—and efficiently respond to—environmental stimuli.[46] These cognitive structures sort, label, and categorize sensory input in ways that lead to appropriate adaptive behaviors. By early adolescence these structures have become stable enough to form what might be called our "general reality orientation"—a preformed set of interpretive categories that efficiently make sense of our daily experience. It is this general reality orientation that structures our ordinary experience of the world. And as valuable as this general reality orientation is for everyday life, it rarely gives us occasion for wonder. The goal of meditation and various spiritual disciplines is to dismantle this general reality orientation and thereby occasion what Fromm called "the wondering, the marveling, the becoming aware of life and of one's own existence, and of the puzzling problem of one's relatedness to the world."

Meditative systems differ widely. They have different goals and utilize different techniques. We can, for example, distinguish between those systems that intensify concentration, those that utilize visualization, those that involve body movement, and those that entail the special form of self-awareness referred to as mindfulness.[47] And it would probably be wrong to suggest that all systems of meditation aim at eliciting wonder. But most do. One of the common aims of

meditative and mystical practices is the deautomatization of the cognitive structures that define profane existence.[48] They do this in many ways. First, they construct environments that minimize exposure to accustomed sensory data: silent rooms, subdued lighting, incense that reduces olfactory awareness to a single sensation, and simply closing one's eyes. All these environmental factors alter the accustomed ratio of incoming sensory data to cognitive processing activities. Second, meditative and mystical practices also try to alter the brain's internal methods of processing sensory information. This is partly accomplished through indoctrination. Newcomers to spiritual disciplines are introduced to beliefs that acknowledge the existence and causal relevance of entities or forces not recognized in the profane world. The brain's cognitive functions are also altered through a combination of physiological (e.g., body movements, drumming, sensory deprivation, ingestion of intoxicating substances that either arouse or dull various neurophysiological processes) and psychological (e.g., visualization, contemplative practice, koans or other mental techniques that induce people to "let go" of habitual cognitive structures) exercises.

Meditation and mystical practices temporarily deactivate a person's accustomed way of experiencing the world. As a result, experience appears novel, fresh, unaccustomed. This alteration in our accustomed ways of making sense of the world introduces the element of surprise—the triggering mechanism for the emotions of curiosity and wonder. Yet, because both physiological and mental activities are typically quiescent during such practices, wonder tends to predominate over curiosity. Claudio Naranjo and Robert Ornstein observe that people who practice meditation typically believe they have discovered dimensions of awareness that are deeper or more profound than the awareness of their normal waking state of consciousness. It is as though they are discovering the very foundations of awareness itself. Meditators commonly report that they "enter states of mind that we may regard as unusual and, at the same time, as the very ground or core of what we consider our ordinary experience. We

would have no such 'ordinary' experience without awareness, for instance, but the intensification of awareness leads us to [an unfamiliar] perspective."[49]

It is precisely such an intensification of awareness and the resulting unfamiliar perspective that elicit the emotion of wonder. Thus, for example, Thich Nhat Hanh, the widely read exponent of Buddhist "mindfulness meditation," describes a variety of exercises aimed at helping people let go of their compulsive mental habits. The goal of mindfulness is to acquire an accepting awareness of whatever arises in the senses. He writes, "I like to walk alone on country paths, rice plants and wild grasses on both sides, putting each foot down on the earth in mindfulness, knowing that I walk on the *wondrous* earth. In such moments, existence is a miraculous and mysterious reality."[50]

There is some scientific evidence to support the claim that meditation and mystical experiences alter neurophysiology in ways that dismantle profane experience and create an occasion for wonder. As we saw in chapter 4, neural imaging studies show that at least some forms of meditation do in fact alter the way that the brain processes sensory information. Herbert Benson was one of the first to demonstrate that meditation has measurable effects on the brain, including the capacity to stimulate blood flow into the limbic system (which plays a large role in generating emotions).[51] Neurologist Andrew Newberg and his colleague Eugene d'Aquili have shown that meditation can temporarily deactivate what they term the "orientation association" region of the brain, thereby facilitating novel sensations of peace and "oneness" with a vaster reality.[52] They also found that certain meditational practices can increase activity in the "attention association" area, creating a flood of novel perceptions that evoke emotional responses. Meanwhile, Richard Davidson has used brain imaging to show that meditation shifts neural activity in the prefontal cortex from one hemisphere to the other—causing people to change from a basic fight-flight orientation to one of calm acceptance.[53] Finally, Dean Hamer suggests that meditation makes use of very specific neurological processes that foster belief in a higher power.[54] While neurological science is not developed enough for us

to understand the exact relationship between brain states and human consciousness, we can at least be certain that meditation and mystical practices are associated with brain states that appear highly conducive to the occasioning of wonder.

The best phenomenological account of the subjective experiences toward which meditation and mystical practices aim is probably to be found in William James's *The Varieties of Religious Experience*. Mystical experiences, James noted, are characterized by their ineffability, noetic quality, transiency, and passivity. That mystical states of consciousness should be largely ineffable is to be expected insofar as they are characterized by the absence of the general reality orientation that ordinarily labels and categorizes experience. James explains that this is why such states "are more like states of feeling than like states of intellect." They are also relatively passive states, states in which people feel "as if their own will were in abeyance, as indeed sometimes as if they were grasped and held by a superior power." They are also transient in that they can rarely be sustained for a very long period of time. Yet the most salient feature of mystical experiences is their pronounced noetic quality. That is, although they don't give rise to the kinds of knowledge arrived at through ordinary rational inquiry, they "seem to those who experience them to be also states of knowledge. . . . They are illuminations, revelations, full of significance and importance, all inarticulate though they remain; and as a rule they carry with them a curious sense of authority for aftertime."[55]

It is important to note that many of the traits that James associates with mystical experience are simultaneously traits of the emotion of wonder. Both are triggered by unexpected perceptions, especially perceptions of particularly vivid instances of beauty, truth, or vitality. Both are states in which the active will seems to be temporarily suspended and the surrounding world appears to be appreciated rather than manipulated. Both alter perception and cognition by prompting consideration of a more general order of things, tending to produce belief in the presence and causal relevance of some reality that lies behind or beyond profane reality.[56] It is thus not surprising

that meditation and mystical practices tend to evoke the emotion of wonder. It is even tempting to suggest that they actually have the evocation of wonder as one of their principal goals. Charles Tart, for example, found that the mystical state resulting from the use of marijuana "characteristically produces a childlike openness to experience and a sense of wonder and awe, in contrast to the usual businesslike manner in which we classify events and people strictly in terms of their importance to us."[57] Religious studies scholar Huston Smith has similarly considered the following account to be a prototypical description of a developed mystical state: "Suddenly I burst into a vast, new, *indescribably wonderful universe*. Although I am writing this over a year later, the *thrill of the surprise and amazement*, the awesomeness of the revelation, the engulfment in an overwhelming feeling-wave of gratitude and *blessed wonderment*, are as fresh, and the memory is as vivid, as if it had happened five minutes ago."[58]

Meditation and mystical practice help usher people into "blessed wonderment." In so doing they make it possible to transcend the profane world, even if only temporarily. Such experiences are transforming. They invigorate life, giving it a zest and resiliency available in no other way. They also make it possible to have what theologian John E. Smith described as a felt sense of the holy ground on which life rests and the consequent ability to arrive at "judgments on life as a whole." Meditation and mystical practice provide avenues through which people might momentarily escape the daily rounds of life, giving us occasion for wonder.

9. Wonder, Emotion, and the Religious Sensibility

The philosopher neutralizes his wonder in ideal
knowledge, while the religious person abides
in that wonder.—MARTIN BUBER

THE RELIGION EDITOR OF A MIDWESTERN NEWSPAPER
recently pondered over what Christmas really meant to him.
He felt restless as the holidays approached. He knew that he
was looking for something, but he was not quite sure what:

> That's when I realized what I was looking for. Wonder. I don't
> mean wonder as in, "I wonder how in the heck I am going to get
> everything done in the next five days." I mean the wonder I felt
> when my bare foot hit the cold carpet as I got out of bed Christ-
> mas morning. The wonder of 500 candles glowing as our church
> sings "Silent Night." The wonder of angels swarming the sky,
> informing a few midnight wanderers their world had changed
> forever. Wonder doesn't do well in the information age. . . . I've
> got way too much information. What I lack is mystery, which is
> where wonder comes from. . . . The Christmas story is one of
> wonder. . . . Whatever one makes of it, it's a moving, mysterious
> lesson [that rekindles] the wonder that makes a child's eyes wide
> and a grownup gasp.[1]

The author of this column, Charles Honey, draws attention to the fact that the myths, doctrines, and rituals of religion—whatever else one makes of them—elicit the experience of wonder. It might even be argued that one of religion's most important functions is to rekindle the wonder that makes a child's eyes wide and a grownup gasp.

This book has drawn on several academic disciplines to describe the origin and function of wonder in human lives. Evolutionary biology, developmental psychology, and historical biography all support the claim that wonder shapes our lives in ways that are broadly spiritual in nature. The words "religion" and "spirituality" are being used interchangeably here, referring to humanity's recurring urge to find greater wholeness by connecting with some reality understood to be more than physical. We have seen, for example, that experiences of wonder prompt us to search for the source of unexpected displays of beauty, order, or vitality in "something more." In the words of theologian John E. Smith, experiences that give occasion for wonder "call forth the sense that beyond and beneath our life is a holy ground."[2] Wonder is thus a stimulus to metaphysical thought. Moreover, it motivates sustained engagement with the world around us. It unleashes our capacities for creative activity and for caring for others in their own right. We should therefore expect a close association between the emotion of wonder and religion. We should also expect that many of us, like Charles Honey, approach religion looking for an infusion of this transforming emotion.

A descriptive analysis of the role of wonder in shaping human lives leads inevitably to a series of questions that become increasingly difficult to answer on descriptive grounds alone: What is the role of emotion in generating a religious orientation to life? How do different discrete emotions affect either the truth or the value of religious beliefs? How does a religious outlook shaped by wonder differ from a religious outlook rooted in other emotions? What forms of religion seem to hamper the expression of wonder? Would we humans be better off, as biologist Richard Dawkins suggests, if we restrained the tendency of wonder to align itself with religion and instead redirected it to scientific pursuits? Put differently, how can we

assess whether wonder guides us to mature and productive relations with the surrounding world?

These may be questions that do not have definitive answers. Yet Charles Honey is right. Religion—whatever one makes of it—is something we turn to when we yearn to rekindle the experience of wonder. It would seem, then, that an informed exploration of the connection between emotion, wonder, and humanity's religious sensibility is warranted even if definitive answers elude us.

Religion and Emotion

The first chapter of this book offered a brief sketch of scholarly discussions of the relationship between religion and emotion. Sigmund Freud, for example, claimed that religion is generated by the emotions of fear, dependency, and guilt. He pointed out that humans find themselves defenseless before the terrors of nature. Disease, natural disasters, and impending death seem to mock at all human control. Even grown adults find themselves yearning for a supernatural being who might protect them. Religious belief, Freud argued, represents the wishful thinking generated by the essentially "negative" emotions of fear and dependency. Freud further pointed out that every culture needs to induce people to repress their antisocial instincts and desires. Cultures do this by producing a sense of guilt and using this guilt to coerce us into conforming to society's moral code. Beliefs about sin, divine judgment, and heavenly rewards or punishments are all examples of how religion is able to manipulate us by taking advantage of our emotional vulnerability. Freud's point, however, was that religious beliefs are illusory. They are based only in subjective emotion—not in objective fact.

Freud argued that the strong hold religion has over people can be traced to the strength of the emotions it feeds on. He viewed religion as a regressive force because the primary emotions that fuel it cut us off from productive relations with the surrounding world. Fear and guilt hinder our acquisition of prudent strategies for coming to terms with the objective world. Freud countered that true progress—

in our personal lives or for civilization as a whole—comes not from emotion but from adopting the kind of problem-solving rationality that has helped science lead the way to cultural progress. Freud contended that we can't take the next step in humanity's cultural evolution until we abandon the illusions of religion and instead adopt a more scientific view of the world.

Freud's critique of religion thus rested, at least in part, on the assumption of a fundamental opposition between emotion and reason. Freud used the term "primary process" to describe the role that emotions play in patterning human behavior. He argued that emotions, in contrast to reason, aim toward immediate personal gratification (either by removing aversive stimuli or producing physiological pleasure). Emotions are essentially selfish, aiming to procure personal gratification without any consideration of others or long-term consequences. Freud further assumed that emotions are blind to the outside world; they are driven wholly by internal forces and are oblivious to the actual workings of the surrounding environment. Freud contrasted all of this with reason, which he proclaimed was governed by the "secondary process" of reflective reason.

Freud's sharp differentiation between reason and emotion has largely been shared by those who have sought to defend religion by arguing for its unique emotional core. Schleiermacher and Otto, for example, both identified emotions that they believed differentiated religion from all other areas of life. Schleiermacher's "feeling of absolute dependence" and Otto's "awe before the holy" were said to constitute sui generis phenomena that grounded religion in its own experiential "data." The truth of religion, they maintained, is anchored in the phenomenological qualities of these specific emotions. Religion, because it is grounded in unique emotions rather than in reason, lies outside the scope of rational criticism.

Most historical studies of religion and emotion have similarly tended to treat emotion as sheer feeling. Analyses of the role of emotion in such phenomena as conversion experiences, Hindu *bhakti*, or medieval mysticism tend to conceptualize emotion as a general category. Emotion is thus typically equated with sentimentality, sub-

jective feeling, and a kind of solipsistic outlook that lacks firm connection with the world outside the self. As a result, discussions of emotion and religion frequently create a forced dichotomy between the role of the heart versus the head, sentiment versus rational calculation.

A truly interdisciplinary look at the origin and function of emotions in human life gives us reason to be wary of the assumptions underlying the arguments typically proposed by both the defenders and detractors of religion. First, we need to understand that emotion cannot be treated as a general category such as sheer feeling. There is no one emotional faculty in the brain. Rather, "the various classes of emotions are mediated by separate neural systems that have evolved for different reasons. If we are interested in understanding the various phenomena that we use the term 'emotion' to refer to, we have to focus on specific classes of emotions."[3]

Second, we also need to keep in mind that natural selection favored emotional systems that govern specific kinds of adaptive behavior. Emotions are "superordinate programs" that regulate behavior in ways that successfully negotiate the many requirements of biological survival (e.g., cooperation, sexual attraction, coalitional aggression, incest avoidance, predator avoidance, investigative scanning of the environment). Stimulus events, either environmental or physiological, trigger emotional programs whose purpose is to mobilize the organism for an appropriate response. This brings us to a third important aspect of emotion: cognition is necessarily entailed in the arousal of emotions. We continually evaluate (often without conscious awareness) the potential harms and benefits existing in the surrounding environment. Emotions are particularly likely to arise in the face of unexpected or uncertain perceptions. Discrepancies between expectations built on past experiences and signals from the present environment create uncertainty, thereby triggering the brains' inherited emotion programs designed to mobilize the organism for appropriate response.

Not only is cognition involved in the arousal of emotions, but emotions mobilize and coordinate a host of perceptual, cognitive,

and behavioral subprograms (e.g., attention, inferences, learning, memory, goal choice, motivational priorities, communication of intention) geared to serve the organism's interests. Emotions therefore "constitute the primary motivational system for human beings" and regulate both cognition and behavior. This is why Robert Solomon has written extensively trying to erase the myth that there is an inherent antithesis between emotion and reason. "Every emotion," he writes, "is a strategy, a purposive attempt to structure our world in such a way as to maximize our sense of personal dignity and self-esteem."[4] Solomon has perhaps overly emphasized the distinctively psychological issues of dignity and self-esteem as opposed to other organismic needs and interests. But his point is well taken. Emotions are adaptive strategies. In humans, emotions seek to maximize subjective measures of well-being and self-worth.

Solomon points out that all emotions are rational in one sense of the word. That is, every emotion is a strategy that aims to maximize our personal survival and prosperity. However, only some emotions are rational in a second sense of the word (i.e., cohering with logical analyses of the actual structure of reality). What prevents most emotions from being rational in the sense of "correspondence with reality" is that most emotions have a magical element. As Sartre put it, emotions are "magical transformations of the world."[5] Emotions seek to reconstitute reality. They do this by reconstituting our orientation to experience in ways that are driven far more by wishful thinking than by reflective analysis of external reality. This is why many emotionally driven behaviors appear pointless to others. After all, emotions often invoke strategies aimed at enhancing our subjective sense of dignity and self-esteem. These strategies may do little to alter the objective environment. Anger or fear, for example, might give rise to such behaviors as kicking, screaming, cursing, or even praying for supernatural powers to smite our enemies. All of these are purposive strategies when viewed from the internal perspective of the acting person but appear pointless to outside observers. Solomon notes that

our desperate emotional expressions often act *as if*—as if the muttered curses and incantations really might have their literal effects ("Go to hell," "May the very heavens strike you . . ."), as if the substitute fetishes and voodoo representations might really transmit some similar results. . . . These irrational beliefs and strategies—particularly when practiced by hard-headed and "rational" people—seem surprising . . . (but to the acting person are) far more important than the impersonal objectivity of rational belief.[6]

The point that most needs to be underscored here is that human beings bring vital needs and interests to their evaluation of, and response to, the surrounding environment. There is no such thing as emotion-free cognition.[7] It is not really a question of *whether* emotions influence our thinking but a matter of *which* emotions most strongly mobilize the subprograms that collectively constitute cognition. Emotions, after all, vary a great deal from one another. They represent very different appraisals of opportunities for gain and loss in relation to one's surroundings. They bring diverse strategies to bear in the organization of perception, cognition, and behavior. Emotions also differ in *the degree to which* they are governed almost solely by subcortical brain structures (and thus relatively hardwired) or are more associated with cortical brain functions (and thus relatively susceptible to influences from experience and conscious deliberation).[8]

The Experience of Wonder and Embodied Spirituality

All these considerations shed light on the role that emotions—and specifically the emotion of wonder—play in shaping our religious sensibilities. A sensibility is a predisposition to perceive, think, and respond to the world in a particular way. Emotions (along with our personal history of environmental reinforcement) are the primary source of all our moods, sensibilities, and traits. Because they mobi-

lize our perceptual and cognitive styles to pursue purposive strategies, emotions shape our personal orientations to the world. Again, it is not an issue of *whether* emotions affect our religious sensibilities but *which* emotions and in *what specific ways*.

The relationship between emotion and religion is a subset of the larger process whereby individuals reconstitute reality in their pursuit of adaptive strategies. A few years ago George Lakoff and Mark Johnson published *Philosophy in the Flesh* to draw attention to the embodied nature of all human thought. Their position was really not new, drawing as it does on neo-Darwinism and the philosophical tradition of American pragmatism. What they succeeded in doing, however, was making a strong case in support of their view that all human thought is "shaped crucially by the peculiarities of our human bodies, by the remarkable details of the neural structure of our brains, and by the specifics of our everyday functioning in the world."[9] It follows that "what we understand the world to be like is determined by many things: our sensory organs, our ability to move and to manipulate objects, the detailed structure of our brain, our culture, and our interactions in the environment, at the very least."[10] To Lakoff and Johnson's list of bodily determinants of thought we must add our emotions and their function as "superordinate programs" affecting motivation, perception, and cognition.

The study of religion and the emotions is, then, a subset of the larger project to understand what might be called "spirituality in the flesh." Indeed, the "body" has become a critical term for understanding religion in contemporary academic circles. Assigned to write the section on the "body" for a recent book highlighting theoretical approaches to the study of religion, William LaFleur observed that "the fact that 'body' has become a critical term for religious studies, whereas 'mysticism,' for instance, has largely dropped out, can itself signal significant change in how we study religion."[11] LaFleur didn't mean that scholars are no longer interested in mysticism. He did, however, wish to underscore that scholars ask new questions about topics such as mysticism and bring new analytic tools to such topics. LaFleur notes, for example, that research on

brain chemistry has established clear connections between neural states and religious experience, making it possible for us to understand what alterations in brain activity are most likely to be experienced as having religious import. He further illustrates how knowledge of the body illuminates the study of religion: "The leverage on our minds exerted by our DNA and what has been called the 'selfish' gene cannot be denied. Studies that reject or ignore such data now seem out-of-date; we have moved from recognizing that religion involves the body to acknowledging, sometimes begrudgingly, that the body is conditioned very powerfully by its own chemistry and biological prehistory."[12]

Recognizing the "leverage" that the body has on religious thought and experience need not divert attention away from the role of culture in constructing human experience. Indeed, the preeminent biologist Edward O. Wilson warns that biological explanations of human behavior can never be complete because, in humans, "genes have given away most of their sovereignty" to culture.[13] Understanding spirituality in the flesh, then, is not about reducing human thought and experience to biology. It is, however, about mapping the anthropological roots of humanity's spiritual impulses. It seeks to explain religion from below (i.e., in terms of human experience) rather than from above (i.e., divine revelation).

A genuinely interdisciplinary study of human spirituality must therefore avail itself of what we know about the motivational functions performed by emotions. To ignore modern understandings of the emotions would, as LaFleur notes, risk appearing out of date. There are, however, at least two reasons why such interdisciplinary investigations must proceed cautiously. First, the scientific study of emotions is still in its early stages. We are a long way from conclusive answers to many of the most basic questions (e.g., separating the roles of nature and nurture, distinguishing between primary and secondary emotions, or identifying the neurophysiological processes involved with specific emotions). It is thus not the case that there is some firm scientific ground from which we can make our forays into the study of religion. Indeed, our very efforts to bring the scientific

study of emotions into dialogue with religious self-consciousness presents interesting possibilities for critically engaging the naturalist assumptions underlying so many of our natural and social sciences. Second, all interpretive efforts implicitly raise the question of what constitutes an explanation. There are at least three levels of any interdisciplinary investigation of human experience: the neurophysiological level (biology), the perceptual-cognitive level (psychology), and the phenomenological level, which consists of the self-consciousness of particular human beings (the history and philosophy of religion). As George Lakoff and Mark Johnson contend, a full understanding of any human experience requires descriptions and explanations at all three levels.[14] Not only does full understanding require explanations at all three levels, but these explanations must also in some fundamental way integrate with one another. This may, in fact, represent something very close to what the philosopher Wilhelm Dilthey had in mind when he distinguished between scientific explanation (*erklaren*) and humanistic understanding (*verstehen*) of human experience. For Dilthey each mode of explanation is empirical. While natural sciences explain experience with reference to causal laws, the human sciences disclose the meanings and values intended by acting persons in their historically constituted situations.[15]

With these cautions in mind, we might now suggest some of the ways that recent studies of the emotions have opened up exciting new ways of understanding religion. We are, for example, now able to move beyond broad generalizations about the relationship between emotion and religion and to formulate new hypotheses about the role that discrete or specific emotions play in religious perception, cognition, or behavior. The importance of identifying discrete emotions does not hinge on the outcome of ongoing debates concerning the number of discrete emotions present at birth as opposed to the number of discrete emotions that are learned over the course of development. Whether innate or learned, discrete emotions mobilize specific kinds of adaptive strategies. For example, some emotions heighten our concern with self-defense and boundary maintenance, while others motivate enhanced rapport and connectedness. Fur-

thermore, some emotions might be considered "negative" in that they mobilize agendas in response to situations in which experience falls short of prior expectations, whereas other emotions are "positive" in that they arise when experience exceeds prior expectations. In addition, some emotions transform reality by seeking to bend external forces (including supernatural entities) to the self, while other emotions bend the self to conform to external realities (including supernatural entities). Thus recent studies of discrete emotions open up a host of exciting possibilities for understanding why, and under what circumstances, humans adopt specific kinds of religious postures toward the world.

For example, fear and anger are prime candidates for further research on how discrete emotions influence the development of religious sensibilities. As Freud has shown, fear mobilizes an essentially defensive posture. Fear typically fosters dependency and "flight" as one's primary orientation to life. Anger, of course, may tip the balance to a "fight" rather than "flight" response—predisposing religious sensibilities to excessive boundary posturing, tribalism, and belligerence. Indeed, a great deal of the boundary posturing and doctrinal rigidity found in North American religious fundamentalism can be traced to the preponderance of the emotions of fear, shame, and anger.[16] Thus, for example, it is clear that there is some relationship between apocalyptic thought and historical circumstances that generate shared feelings of helplessness, anger, and shame. This is especially true when those struggling to adhere to inherited beliefs find themselves relegated to secondary social and economic status even while the wider culture is seemingly prospering. Beleaguered religious communities understandably come to feel anger toward those who jeopardize their social boundaries and in all likelihood experience some level of shame insofar as they recognize that the temptation to apostasy resides even within themselves.[17] Research on the motivational functions of discrete emotions shows that "fear provides an excellent example of the power of emotion to organize and direct perceptual and cognitive processes. Fear tends to produce 'tunnel vision' by focusing attention on the source of the

threat and restricting cue utilization. Keen attention to the threatening agent or situation can be adaptive in guiding self-protective behavior. Such restrictions on attentional processes in unrealistic or unwarranted fear are maladaptive."[18]

The "tunnel vision" produced by fear might well explain why some fundamentalist communities are prone to forms of apocalyptic thought that focus attention on threatening "signs of the times" as a cue to the presence of supernatural enemies such as Satan or the Antichrist. Fear (especially when this is fear is partially generated by one's own internal impulses to stray from the narrow truth) can breed an obsession with viewing one's world as fraught with religious danger, rendering people incapable of entering into productive relationships with the surrounding world. The same, of course, is true of emotions such as anger that tend to produce antisocial aggression. Thus "a challenge to one's ego or self-esteem that increases attention to the self may activate a pattern in which shame precedes, activates, and amplified anger. In individuals with spuriously high self-esteem, this pattern greatly increases the likelihood of aggression and violence."[19] We need to know more about why religions so often encourage the expression of such potentially maladaptive human tendencies. Of particular interest would be new historical and comparative studies that could shed light on how religious traditions might regulate and redirect the expression of these emotions in ways that promote long-term adaptive behaviors. Given religion's role in the culture wars that divide our planet, we cannot afford the luxury of ignoring what the natural and social sciences can tell us about "spirituality in the flesh."

We should expect that a religious sensibility shaped by the experience of wonder will differ dramatically from those shaped primarily by shame, guilt, or fear. It is for this reason that the preceding chapters can be understood as making an important contribution to an overall understanding of "spirituality in the flesh." The experience of wonder exerts a certain leverage on humans' everyday functioning in the world. There are, as we have seen, prototypical patterns according to which wonder reconstitutes reality in the pursuit of adaptive

strategies. For example, experiences of wonder typically lead to "enhanced rapport" rather than to defensive maneuvering and avoidance. From a perceptual standpoint, wonder makes attending to objects in their own right intrinsically rewarding. From a cognitive standpoint, wonder fosters "accommodation" over assimilation, prompting us to modify our previous cognitive structures to include the ever widening contours of the environment as opposed to incorporating new experiences into the existing stock of ideas with which we fashion instrumental behavior. These changes help us to bring otherwise distant people and objects into our personal scheme of ends, helping us to have empathy and concern for the wider world. And, by prompting us to detect causal agencies that lie somehow behind or beyond observed events, wonder predisposes us to religious and metaphysical thought.

It would seem that wonder, considered as a prototypical category of human experience, predisposes us to a religious sensibility something along the lines of what historian William Clebsch has termed an "esthetic spirituality." Clebsch's term is meant to draw our attention to a form of spirituality based not on obedience to transcendent authority but rather on a distinct mode of apprehending experience. According to Clebsch, an aesthetic spirituality is rooted in "a consciousness of the beauty of living in harmony with divine things—in a word, being at home in the universe."[20] This definition would surely fit the religious sensibilities discernible in the lives of John Muir, William James, and Rachel Carson. In fact, Clebsch identified James—along with the Puritan theologian Jonathan Edwards and the Transcendentalist visionary Ralph Waldo Emerson—as one of the three clearest examples of this spiritual style in American history. Muir, James, and Carson were all moved by wonder to view occurrences as a wonder. Their sensibility for the "more" of experience led to a spirituality centered in not doctrine per se but in the intrinsic delight accompanying experiences "of the beauty of living in harmony with divine things." Emerson's life and thought also neatly conform to this category of wonder-driven aesthetic spirituality. We might remember that Muir was introduced first to Emerson's writings, and then

Emerson personally, by Ezra and Jeanne Carr. This, of course, suggests that we are far from possessing a full understanding of the interplay between biological and cultural sources of emotional experience. This is also why the life and thought of someone like Jonathan Edwards remain an excellent counterexample to the seeming symmetry between the experience of wonder and what we are calling aesthetic spirituality. Historians such as William Clebsch and Perry Miller have long puzzled over how someone like Jonathan Edwards—who almost surely had vivid experiences of wonder—resisted the cognitive tendencies usually associated with wonder and retained the conservative, doctrinally based religious orientation of his Puritan heritage.[21] Thus for all the knowledge we now have about the "leverage" that the body brings to human religiosity, we still have much to learn about the relationship between religion and the emotions.

Trying to explain human religiosity from the perspective of the body's adaptive mechanisms raises a host of questions. We might, for example, ask what sets of circumstances are most likely to elicit a wonder-driven religious sensibility. We have repeatedly noted that emotional experiences most often arise in response to unexpected perceptions. In the case of wonder this frequently includes extraordinary displays of beauty, order, and vitality. This is undoubtedly why Muir, James, and Carson were particularly prone to such experiences when surrounded by nature or in the presence of something uncanny such as ostensible instances of "paranormal" phenomena. Both the grandeur of natural landscapes and paranormal phenomena defy explanation according to our acquired notions of causality, hence sending the mind in search of some causal agency that must lie just behind or beyond sensory experience. Human-made artifacts, no matter how grand, are less likely to defy customary notions of causality and are hence also less likely to arouse experiences of wonder. Yet, as Charles Honey noted, religious rituals frequently prove capable of widening a child's eyes and making a grownup gasp. Mystery and the expectation of supernatural activity engage our attention and draw us into states of reverie and wonder. However, not all religious communities value mystery and the open-ended cognitive

hypotheses that it might spontaneously engender. It is quite possible, in fact, that many religious communities espouse worldviews that prompt them to discourage the evocation of wonder and the adaptive strategies that it typically sets into motion.

To summarize, the experience of wonder is a recurring feature of humanity's interaction with the surrounding world. As with all embodied experiences, its origin can be described with reference to the peculiarities of our human bodies, by the remarkable details of the neural structure of our brains, and to the specifics of our everyday functioning in the world (inclusive of the role of culture in constructing those everyday functions). Knowing something about the biology and psychology of a wonder-based religious sensibility would thus appear extremely relevant to the contemporary study of religion. As LaFleur explained, we have moved from recognizing that religion involves the body to acknowledging, sometimes begrudgingly, that the body is conditioned very powerfully by its own chemistry and biological prehistory. But this acknowledgment in and of itself doesn't begin to resolve the many issues that arise in the study of religion. It is thus important that we conclude our study by attempting—however tentatively—to move beyond a description of the biological and psychological patterning of wonder to a broader assessment of its place in a religious orientation to life.

Wonder and Religion: Evoking an Unseen Order

Early in *The Varieties of Religious Experience*, William James observes that people become religious in direct proportion to their experience of what he calls "the reality of the unseen." James states that if asked "to characterize the life of religion in the broadest and most general terms possible, one might say that it consists of the belief that there is an unseen order, and that our supreme good lies in harmoniously adjusting ourselves thereto."[22] Wonder, as we have seen, is one of the brain's hardwired programs that respond to unexpected phenomena. Unlike other emotional systems, however, wonder seeks the causal agency responsible for these phenomena at a level that exists

somehow behind or above observed reality. For this reason wonder is one of the principal sources of belief in an unseen order. Experiences of wonder have long-lasting effects on our moods, motivations, and attitudes. They shape a very distinctive religious sensibility. As James explains, not just our religious attitudes but all our attitudes are created in response "to the 'objects' of our consciousness, the things which we believe to exist, whether really or ideally, along with ourselves. Such objects may be present to our senses, or they may be present only to our thought. In either case they elicit from us a reaction."[23]

James's point is that someone is religious in direct proportion to her or his felt sense of an unseen order of life. We possess a spiritual sensibility to the degree that our perceptual and cognitive systems are predisposed to acknowledge this unseen order as an object of our consciousness. This, of course, is precisely the function that wonder performs in shaping our strategic orientation to the world. Wonder emerges in response to novel or unexpected stimuli. It engages cognitive activities that are predisposed to grant ontological reality to an order of existence that somehow lies behind, beyond, or at a more general level of existence. The cognitive states most closely associated with wonder appear to constitute what James had in mind when he accounted for the emergence of such belief in an unseen order. James wrote that is "as if there were in the human consciousness *a sense of reality, a feeling of objective presence, a perception* of what we may call 'something there,' . . . a sense of present reality more diffused and general than that which our special senses yield."[24]

It is, of course, the special function of wonder to create such a feeling of the objective presence of something "more." Yet the fact that wonder predisposes us toward belief in the existence of an unseen order does not help us decide whether such belief is psychologically healthy. All too often wonder encourages sheer credulity. This chapter opened with Charles Honey's recollection of how Christmas songs and candles prompt thought of angels swarming the sky heralding the birth of Christ. In India, however, temple icons prompt thought of the supernatural assistance available to us from the

elephant-headed deity Ganesha. Yet in China, otherwise inexplicable events are attributed to the causal power wielded by the spirits of one's ancestors. Wonder, it seems, is capable of encouraging belief in a wide variety of supernatural agencies. As James observed, "Such is the ontological imagination, and such is the convincingness of what it brings to birth. Unpicturable beings are realized, and realized with an intensity almost like that of an hallucination."[25] Our wonder-driven imaginations are easily molded by religious and cultural traditions. The existence of social reference groups that attest to the truth of these traditions give even greater convincingness to the existence of these unpicturable beings.

Creating mental images of what "possibly" exists is an indispensable part of higher-order human cognition. What is difficult, however, is discerning the limits of such possibility. It is all but impossible to refine wonder-driven mental constructs through the kind of active experimentation we use to verify hypotheses concerning the world that is palpably "out there." We simply do not receive the same kind of direct environmental feedback to help us adjudicate between competing cognitive constructions as we do when we restrict ourselves to sensory objects only. We are often left with no other measure of the probable truth of our conceptions than our culture's prevailing religious traditions.

The epistemological limits of wonder-driven thought do not, however, merit considering it a quaint but useless misdirection of cognitive potentials that were actually designed for more immediate, adaptively useful epistemic purposes.[26] Imagining the possible is the seed of humanity's loftiest intellectual achievements (e.g., the conception of universal human rights, visions of social justice, convictions of the intrinsic worth of future generations and the ecological claims they put on us—the last of which could not be more clearly evidenced than in the lives and thought of John Muir, William James, and Rachel Carson). Among other things, this capacity to envision more general orders of existence makes it possible for us to behold our world as a universe rather than a disconnected pluriverse. It also makes it possible to speak of intrinsic meanings and values. The chief

difference between humans and other species is not that we are less emotional than they are; it is, rather, the rich exuberant excess of the possibilities we entertain—possibilities generated by the direction that emotions exert on our perception and cognition. If we allow the pursuit of scientific materialism to pare down our construction of possible orders of existence to what is objectively "out there" or immediately expedient, we will thwart the development of our loftiest intellectual potentials.[27]

Of all human emotions, then, it seems that wonder is most likely to shape sensibilities geared to orient individuals to the broadest range of experience and to discern what experience testifies to be its ultimate context. Wonder infuses consciousness with a sense of reality, a feeling of objective presence, a perception of "something there" that is more diffused and more general than that which our physical senses yield. Wonder incites belief in the reality of the unseen. And whether this unseen exists really or only to our thought, it nonetheless elicits existential and ethical responses wholly unlike those that would characterize a life devoid of sensibilities stimulated by wonder.

Wonder and Religion: A Final Assessment

We have seen how experiences of wonder have a natural tendency to evoke belief in an unseen order of things. We have not, however, yet raised the issue of how a wonder-driven religious sensibility is to be evaluated. Matters of evaluation are not strictly descriptive. They entail normative judgment. What criteria are available to us to evaluate emotional experiences? How do we decide whether a life shaped by wonder is to be preferred over a life relatively devoid of this emotion? How can we assess the relative strengths and weaknesses of wonder as a basic orientation toward life? Where do we turn for criteria according to which we might decide whether to approve or disapprove of the religious tendencies so often associated with experiences of wonder?

It is helpful in this regard to draw once again on the sage advice of William James. A little more than a hundred years ago James found

himself in the position of trying to evaluate the many varieties of religious experience. As a philosopher and psychologist, he could not use criteria drawn from scripturally based theologies. He instead sought criteria that weren't specific to any one religious institution. He concluded that the criteria must concern not the purported truth of religious experiences but rather their pragmatic value in nourishing life in ways that square with commonly accepted conceptions of psychological health. James reasoned that efforts to evaluate religious sensibilities must be based on "what we can ascertain of their experiential relations to our moral needs and to the rest of what we hold as true. *Immediate luminousness*, in short, *philosophical reasonableness*, and *moral helpfulness* are the only available criteria."[28] These are pragmatic criteria. They are meant to gauge the extent to which a particular religious sensibility enhances—or constrains—humanity's pursuit of the widest possible range of objective and subjective satisfactions. And for this reason they are criteria that can guide interdisciplinary investigations of the overall value of emotional experiences.

That wonder, if even for the briefest duration of time, expands our range of subjective richness is alone warrant for considering it among humanity's most sublime emotions. Its value to human life can be justified on this criterion alone. Experiences of wonder arrest our active will. They make possible the quiet contemplation of a grander scheme of life that strikes us as responsible for life's beauty, order, and vitality. Wonder thereby evokes the subjective sense that we have established a harmonious relationship with the widest possible range of human experience. Wonder is thus accompanied by joy and by feelings of expansiveness. Our lives seem to open up to new possibilities. John Muir, for example, was moved to believe that that our natural universe is open to the Divine Soul. His experiences in nature filled him with "rejoicing and wondering." He was moved to contemplate the possible existence of not yet understood forces present within nature and within ourselves—forces capable of producing incidents of clairvoyance and telepathy. James, too, was moved by his wonder-driven experiences to conclude that "there are resources in

us that naturalism with its literal and legal virtues never recks of, possibilities that take our breath away, of another kind of happiness and power, based on giving up our own will and letting something higher work for us."[29] Experiences of wonder open up the realm of possibility, making us feel continuous with sources of beauty, order, and vitality unexpected in a purely rational approach to life. All of this makes for experiences of "immediate luminousness." There can be no question but that they have an immediate subjective feel that strikes us as rewarding in their own right without further need for outside evaluation.

The subjective feeling of an emotional experience is not, however, itself sufficient to establish its overall pragmatic value. An emotional experience (and the religious sensibility to which it might give rise) must also comport with "the rest of what we hold as true." In other words, it must also meet our second pragmatic criterion, philosophical reasonableness. True, most biological and psychological researchers equate wonder-driven cognition with mistaken notions about cause and effect. Richard Dawkins speaks for many who hold a strong version of evolutionary psychology when he argues that we have an appetite for wonder, an appetite that "real science" ought to be feeding, not religion. This would also be true of most developmental psychologists who assume that the cognitive forms associated with experiences of wonder will gradually be discarded in the movement toward adult rationality. Yet, when viewed from another perspective, wonder can be seen as one of the emotional sources of humanity's highest cognitive achievements. Cognitive development also requires the construction of realms of possibility. Much of adult life requires our ability to formulate conceptions of more general orders of life in terms of which specific events or behaviors can be assigned meaning and value. Indeed, the highest conceptions of justice, dignity, and worth all require highly developed notions of a general order of existence that in some fundamental way lies "beyond" the observed parts of life. The important point here is that philosophical claims accompanying wonder must be assessed ac-

cording to standards derived from enhanced accommodation to—not assimilation of—the wider environments we inhabit.

Experiences of wonder may, in fact, open up certain kinds of realities that are not available to other kinds of rationality. For example, Martin Buber defended the notion that human life is impoverished if we are restricted solely to I-It relationships. He explained that if we wish to experience the eternal "Thou," we must abandon secular rationality and instead learn to "receive an occurrence as a 'wonder.'"[30] Buber acknowledged that both the philosopher and the religious person wonder at phenomena but "the one neutralizes his wonder in ideal knowledge, while the other abides in that wonder."[31] Buber's point is that some of life's deepest meanings remain closed to us if we "neutralize" wonder by insisting, like Dawkins, that it must immediately conform to the epistemological contours of secular materialism.

Any assessment of the relationship between experiences of wonder and "the rest of what we hold as true" must be prepared to acknowledge that wonder-driven cognition is rife with magical qualities. This is, of course, problematic from a philosophical perspective. When assessed according to the criterion of enhanced assimilation, magical thinking appears to be an immature and irrational cognitive orientation to the world. Magical thinking thwarts the assimilation of experience into a developing repertoire of "working conceptions" of the world. Yet cognitive psychologists have recognized that magical thinking is potentially valuable when considered from the standpoint of enhanced accommodation to experience.[32] Magical thinking involves a blurring of the usual boundary between the "inner self" and the "external world." This allows individuals to feel a basic symmetry between their inner life (i.e., thoughts and desires) and the surrounding world. Wonder, and the magical blurring of distinct boundaries it sometimes occasions, thus promote certain mental dispositions conducive to psychological well-being: a sense of seamless continuity with the world, felt participation in a larger whole, relatedness to things of meaning, having a sense of control over life,

and basic trust that the universe is responsive to our needs and desires. The point here is that magical thinking has some adaptive qualities. While it is not philosophically reasonable to live permanently in a world with such blurred boundaries, it is quite reasonable to strive for a life that periodically benefits from the affiliative nature of wondrous experience.

It appears, then, that even the elements of fantasy and illusion to which wonder often leads have some trace of philosophical reasonableness. But this is not to say that abiding in wonder alone is an appropriate orientation to life. Without the balancing emotion of curiosity, wonder will eventually lead to unproductive relationships with the world. As Piaget discovered, curiosity, too, arises amid unexpected perceptions. Curiosity turns cognition toward the ever smaller parts that make up the totality of experience. Curiosity guides the process whereby we fine-tune ideas so that they better correspond with things as they are, independent of our desires and wishes. It is curiosity, not wonder, that puts us into working touch with reality and ensures the development of productive relationships with the world over the long run. We must conclude, therefore, that unbalanced by critical reason, experiences of wonder can lead to sheer credulity. There is no philosophical merit in continuous preoccupation with nonexistent fantasies or illusions. Thus any final judgment of the philosophical reasonableness of emotional experiences such as wonder must conclude that abiding in wonder alone is never an appropriate philosophical response to life.

This leads us to one final issue concerning the philosophical reasonableness of wonder-driven cognition. While it is true that wonder-driven thought carries some philosophical risk, so, too, does thought that is wholly devoid of wonder. This is particularly true of systems of thought that are overtly religious or theological in nature—yet lack any element of wonder. Wonder imparts a heuristic quality to cognition. It leads us forward, inviting us to discover more. Experiences of wonder seem to reveal an intrinsic value to life around us. In this way they draw us out, leading us to seek a more intimate or harmonious relationship with our surroundings. To this extent a

religious sensibility shaped by wonder has a leading or heuristic quality—a quality that arguably separates mature from immature forms of religious thinking.[33] Wonder instills fascination with its object yet recognizes that this object in some fundamental way eludes literal designation. We might be reminded here of Rachel Carson's confession that wonder incited in her a passion for "some universal truth that lies just beyond our grasp. . . . [a meaning that] haunts and ever eludes us, and in its very pursuit we approach the ultimate mystery of Life."[34] Wonder, then, potentially wards off literalism in religious thought (as well as the authoritarianism that so often accompanies literalism). This is a particularly important point because, as Marjorie Taylor and Stephanie Carlson have found, some religious groups actively suppress the kind of cognitive openness generated by wonder.[35] Many conservative religious communities suppress nonlinear thought because it violates their clear bifurcation of the secular and sacred. This gap separating humans from the sacred, they maintain, cannot be bridged from the human side—leaving us dependent on the mediating functions performed for us through scriptural or ecclesiastical authority. Assuming that mature spirituality ought to enliven rather than deaden the human intellect, some degree of wonder is indispensable to philosophically reasonable religious thought.

We might now turn to the connection between experiences of wonder and our third pragmatic criterion, their relationship to our moral needs. Wonder, like joy and interest, is characterized by its rare ability to elicit prolonged engagement with life. Experiences of wonder succeed in motivating creative and constructive approaches to life by imbuing the surrounding world with an alluring luster. Experiences of wonder enable us to view the world independent of its relationships to our own immediate needs. They thereby foster empathy and compassion. It is true that wonder per se is likely to issue in contemplation rather than immediate action. Yet, as we saw in the lives of Muir, James, and Carson, this is not to suggest that wonder leads to passivity or an evasion of moral responsibility. Their lives provide ample evidence that experiences of wonder pull into our

own circle of concerns objects that would otherwise be of remote interest. As De Pascuale points out, an experience of wonder "brings the world into relief and makes a person take life seriously. In wonder you realize that this is it. You have the opportunity to swim through the river of life rather than just float on it, to own your life rather than be owned by it."[36] Wonder alters perception in such a way that we are afforded a new chance to choose how to be—to become true individuals and true citizens of the universe. Assessed for their "moral helpfulness," then, experiences of wonder would seem uniquely capable of luring us into what Rachel Carson called a reverence for life.

Experiences of wonder would thus seem to comport well with reasonable criteria for healthy and responsible living. Such experiences, moreover, often give rise to an enduring sensibility for an unseen order of life—a sensibility that also fares well when assessed for its immediate luminousness, philosophical reasonableness, and moral helpfulness. Of course, wonder alone cannot sustain productive relationships with the surrounding world over the long run. It is true that wonder doesn't mobilize perception or cognition in ways that conform to the requirements of physical survival. It is also true that we can efficiently go through life without delighting in experiences of wonder. Many people do. But it must also be emphasized that no other emotion so effectively induces us to pause, admire, and open our hearts and minds. No other emotion so readily kindles a reverence for life. And thus although you can surely go through life without a developed sense of wonder, it is equally true that a life shaped by wonder is attuned to the widest possible world of personal fulfillment.

NOTES

Chapter 1

1 Friedrich Schleiermacher, *On Religion: Speeches to Its Cultured Despisers*, trans. John Oman (New York: Harper and Brothers, 1958), 82.

2 Ibid., 79.

3 Rudolf Otto, *The Idea of the Holy*, trans. John Harvey (New York: Oxford University Press, 1958), 36.

4 Sigmund Freud, *Civilization and Its Discontents*, trans. John Strachey (New York: W. W. Norton, 1961), 81. Freud also developed his argument concerning the role of guilt in religion in his somewhat obscure text *Moses and Monotheism* (New York: Knopf, 1939). His best explanation of how the emotions of helplessness, dependency, and fear give rise to religious belief is in *The Future of an Illusion* (Garden City, N.Y.: Anchor Books, 1961).

5 See John Corrigan, "History, Religion, and Emotion: A Historiographical Survey," app. 1 in *Business of the Heart: Religion and Emotion in the Nineteenth Century* (Berkeley: University of California Press, 2002), 269–80. Corrigan's essay is one of the best overviews of scholarly inquiries into the relationship between religion and the emotions. His summary and bibliographical citations inform the next several pages of this chapter. See also John Corrigan, ed., *Religion and Emotion: Approaches and Interpretations* (New York: Oxford University Press, 2004), and John Corrigan, Eric Crump, and John Kloos, *Emotion and Religion: A Critical Assessment and Annotated Bibliography* (Westport, Conn.: Greenwood Press, 2000). Another excellent discussion of emotion and a specific religious tradition (Buddhism) can be found in a special collection of articles, "Ethics and Emotions in South Asian Buddhism," in the *Journal of the American Academy of Religion* 71 (September 2003).

6 See Peter N. Stearns and Carol Z. Stearns, "Emotionology: Clarifying the

History of Emotions and Emotional Standards," *American Historical Review* 90 (October 1985): 813–36.

7   See the extended discussion of hatred in apocalyptic religious thought in Robert C. Fuller, *Naming the Antichrist: The History of an American Obsession* (New York: Oxford University Press, 1995).

8   See such studies as Arjun Appadurai, "Topographies of the Self: Praise and Emotion in Hindu India," in *Language and the Politics of Emotion*, ed. Catherine Lutz and Lila Abud-Lughod (Cambridge, England: Cambridge University Press, 1990), 92–112; Harvey Aronson, *Love and Sympathy in Theravada Buddhism* (Delhi: Motilal Barasidass, 1980); Krishna Sharma, *Bhakti and the Bhakti Movement: A Study in the History of Ideas* (New Delhi: Munshiram Manaharlal Publishers, 1987); June McDaniel, *The Madness of the Saints: Ecstatic Religion in Bengal* (Chicago: University of Chicago Press, 1989); Andrew Rawlinson, "Love and Meditation in the Bhakti Tradition," in *The Saints: Studies in a Devotional Tradition of India*, ed. Karine Schomer and W. H. McLeod (Berkeley: University of California Press, 1987), 53–58; and Jean LeCler, *Monks and Love in Twelfth-Century France: A Psychohistorical Essay* (Oxford: University of Oxford Press, 1979).

9   C. Gispert-Sauch, *Bliss in the Upanishads: An Analytical Study of the Origin and Growth of the Vedic Concept of Ananda* (New Delhi: Orientalia Publishers, 1977).

10   Corrigan, *Business of the Heart*, 280.

11   This observation about the emotion of wonder comes from a talk that religious studies scholar Kelly Bulkeley gave at the November 2002 meeting of the American Academy of Religion titled "The Evolution of Wonder: Religious and Neuroscientific Perspectives."

12   See Robert Plutchik, *Emotions and Life: Perspectives from Psychology, Biology, and Evolution* (Washington, D.C.: American Psychological Association, 2003), 73.

13   René Descartes, *The Passions of the Soul*, trans. Stephen Voss (Indianapolis, Ind.: Hackett Publishing, 1989), 307. One of Descartes's translators, Norman Kemp Smith, notes that Descartes used the French word *l'admiration*, for which "wonder" is the closest English equivalent; the only possible alternatives to "wonder" are the English words "surprise," "interest," or "concern." See Norman Kemp Smith, trans., *Descartes' Philosophical Writings* (London: Macmillan, 1952), 306.

14   Descartes, *Passions of the Soul*.

15   The *Natyashastra* originally listed eight *rasas* (emotions); the ninth (*shanta*, or peace or serenity) was added in the eighth century C.E. and has been accepted as a basic emotion ever since. An excellent recent study of

this topic can be found in Susan Schwartz, *Rasa* (New York: Columbia University Press, 2004). Schwartz notes that, according to the *Natya-shastra*, the very purpose of the arts is to offer access to "devotion and wonder" (2). Additional insight into the role of emotions in traditional Indian aesthetics can be found in A. L. Basham, *The Wonder That Was India* (New York: Grove Press, 1954) and René Daumal, *Rasa, or Knowledge of the Self* (New York: New Directions Books, 1982).

16 See the helpful discussion of the "Rasadhaya" in Richard A. Shweder and Jonathan Haidt, "The Cultural Psychology of the Emotions: Ancient and New," in *Handbook of Emotions*, 2nd ed., ed. Michael Lewis and Jeannette M. Haviland-Jones (New York: Guilford Press, 2000), 397–416.

17 An excellent discussion of the Indian notion of *darshan* can be found in Diana Eck, *Darsan: Seeing the Divine Image in India* (New York: Columbia University Press, 1998).

18 Carroll Izard and Brian Ackerman, "Motivational, Organizational, and Regulatory Functions of Discrete Emotions," in Lewis and Haviland-Jones, *Handbook of Emotions*, 257.

19 This observation about the adaptive function of receptive modes of perception (such as wonder) comes from Don Browning, *The Moral Context of Pastoral Care* (Philadelphia: Westminster Press, 1976).

20 Martha Nussbaum, *Upheavals of Thought: The Intelligence of Emotions* (Cambridge, England: Cambridge University Press, 2001).

21 William James, *The Varieties of Religious Experience* (Cambridge, Mass.: Harvard University Press, 1985), 51.

22 Ibid., 55, 59; emphasis in original.

Chapter 2

1 Paul Ekman provides an excellent overview of Darwin's approach to the study of the emotions in his introductory essay that accompanies Charles Darwin, *The Expression of the Emotions in Man and Animals* (London: HarperCollins, 1998).

2 A succinct summary of Darwin's evolutionary account of the emotions can be found in Robert Plutchik, *Emotions and Life: Perspectives from Psychology, Biology, and Evolution* (Washington, D.C.: American Psychological Association, 2003), 24–29.

3 Darwin, *Expression of the Emotions in Man and Animals*, 34.

4 Ibid.

5 Ibid.

6 Ibid., 99–100.

7 See B. F. Skinner, *The Behavior of Organisms* (New York: Appleton-

Century-Crofts, 1939), 407–9, and *About Behaviorism* (New York: Knopf, 1974), 152–70.

8   Stanley Schachter and Jerome Singer, "Cognitive, Social, and Physiological Determinants of Emotional States," *Psychological Review* 69 (September 1962): 379–99. Carroll Izard provides a helpful summary and critique of Schachter and Singer's experiment in his *Human Emotions* (New York: Plenum Press, 1977), 32–34.

9   Volney Gay provides a helpful assessment of the constructivist versus biological approaches to the study of emotions in the *Journal of the American Academy of Religion*'s special issue titled "Ethics and Emotions in South Asian Buddhism." See Volney Gay, "Passionate about Buddhism: Contesting Theories of Emotion," *Journal of the American Academy of Religion* 71 (September 2003): 605–14.

10 Rom Harré, ed., *The Social Construction of Emotions* (Oxford, England: Blackwell, 1986), 6.

11 Ibid.

12 Joseph LeDoux, *The Emotional Brain* (New York: Simon and Schuster, 1996), 137.

13 Robert Plutchik provides an overview of the evolutionary approach to the study of emotions in his essay "The Circumplex as a General Model of the Structures of Emotion and Personality," in *Circumplex Models of Personality and Emotions*, ed. Robert Plutchik and Hope Conte (Washington, D.C.: American Psychological Association, 1997), 17–46.

14 Leda Cosmides and John Tooby, "Evolutionary Psychology and the Emotions," in *Handbook of Emotions*, 2nd ed., ed. Michael Lewis and Jeannette M. Haviland-Jones (New York: Guilford Press, 2000), 91–115.

15 Ibid., 100.

16 Aaron Ben-Ze'ev, *The Subtlety of Emotions* (Cambridge, Mass.: MIT Press, 2000), xiii. Among other recent summaries of theoretical difficulties in the study of emotions are the first two chapters in Plutchik, *Emotions and Life*; the preface and introduction to Keith Oatley and Jennifer Jenkins, *Understanding Emotions* (Malden, Mass.: Blackwell, 1996); and the first eight essays in Lewis and Haviland-Jones, *Handbook of Emotions*.

17 See Plutchik, *Emotions and Life*, 106.

18 See Richard Lazarus, *Emotion and Adaptation* (New York: Oxford University Press, 1991).

19 Izard, *Human Emotions*, 3.

20 Cosmides and Tooby, "Evolutionary Psychology and the Emotions," 103–11.

21 See Paul Ekman, *Emotion in the Human Face*, 2nd ed. (Cambridge, England: Cambridge University Press, 1982); Paul Ekman, "Strong Evidence

for Universals in Facial expressions," *Psychological Bulletin* 115 (March 1994): 268–87; Carroll Izard, *The Psychology of Emotions* (New York: Plenum Press, 1991); and Carroll Izard, "Facial Expressions and the Regulation of Emotions," *Personality and Social Psychology* 58 (March 1990): 487–98.

22 Gay, "Passionate about Buddhism," 606.

23 Ibid., 607.

24 Richard A. Shweder and Jonathan Haidt, "The Cultural Psychology of the Emotions: Ancient and New," in Lewis and Haviland-Jones, *Handbook of Emotions*, 397–416.

25 René Descartes, *The Passions of the Soul*, trans. Stephen Voss (Indianapolis, Ind.: Hackett Publishing, 1989).

26 Plutchik, *Emotions and Life*, 73.

27 Ben-Ze'ev, *Subtlety of Emotions*, 6.

28 Jonathan Haidt, "The Moral Emotions," in *Handbook of Affective Sciences*, ed. Richard J. Davidson, Klaus Scherer, and H. Hill Goldsmith (New York: Oxford University Press, 2003), 852–70.

29 Ibid., 863.

30 Nico Frijda, *The Emotions* (Cambridge, England: Cambridge University Press, 1986), 18.

31 Haidt, "Moral Emotions," 863.

32 Richard Lazarus and Bernice Lazarus, *Passion and Reason: Making Sense of Our Emotions* (New York: Oxford University Press, 1994), 129.

33 Ibid., 135.

34 Ibid., 136.

35 LeDoux, *Emotional Brain*, 16.

36 Darwin, *Expression of the Emotions in Man and Animals*, 278.

37 Ibid., 284; emphasis added.

38 See Sylvan Tomkins, *Affect, Imagery, Consciousness*, vol. 1 (New York: Springer, 1962), and Sylvan Tomkins, "Affect as the Primary Motivational System," in *Feelings and Emotions*, ed. M. Arnold (New York: Academic Press, 1970), 101–10.

39 Carroll Izard and Brian Ackerman, "Motivational, Organizational, and Regulatory Functions of Discrete Emotions," in Lewis and Haviland-Jones, *Handbook of Emotions*, 258.

40 Ibid., 257.

41 A helpful overview of the neurological basis of emotions can be found in Plutchik, *Emotions and Life*, 261–91. Other introductions to the neurophysiology of emotions include Joseph LeDoux and Elizabeth Phelps, "Emotional Networks in the Brain," in Lewis and Haviland-Jones, *Handbook of Emotions*, 157–72; John Cacioppo, Gary Bernston, Jeff Larsen,

Kirsten Poehlmann, and Tiffany Ito, "The Psychophysiology of Emotion," in Lewis and Haviland-Jones, *Handbook of Emotions*, 173–92; and Richard Lane and Lynn Nadel, eds., *Cognitive Neuroscience of Emotion* (New York: Oxford University Press, 2000).

42 See John Aggleton and Andrew Young, "The Enigma of the Amygdala: On Its Contribution to Human Emotion," in Lane and Nadel, *Cognitive Neuroscience of Emotion*, 106–28.

43 Kelly Bulkeley, "The Evolution of Wonder: Religious and Neuroscientific Perspectives," paper delivered at the November 2002 meeting of the American Academy of Religion. Professor Bulkeley expanded on the relevance of cognitive neuroscience to the study of religion in "The Gospel According to Darwin," *Religious Studies Review* 29 (April 2003): 123–30.

44 E. R. Kandel, J. H. Schwartz, and T. M. Jessel, eds., *Principles of Neural Science* (New York: McGraw-Hill, 2000), 349.

45 Bulkeley, "Evolution of Wonder."

46 Ibid.

Chapter 3

1 In their readable and helpful introductory text *Understanding Emotions* (Malden, Mass.: Blackwell, 1996), Keith Oatley and Jennifer Jenkins provide a useful discussion of "the affective realm: emotions—moods—dispositions" (124–30). In brief, they suggest that although most emotional experiences are episodes that last from a few seconds to a few minutes, moods "are relatively long-lasting emotional states," and personality traits or dispositions clearly have "an emotional component." See also the discussion of the relationship between feeling and emotion in Antonio Damasio, "A Note on the Neurobiology of Emotions," in *Altruism and Altruistic Love: Science, Philosophy, and Religion in Dialogue*, ed. Stephen Post, Lynn Underwood, Jeffrey Schloss, and William Hurlbut (New York: Oxford University Press, 2002), 264–71.

2 Juan De Pascuale, "A Wonder Full Life," *Notre Dame Magazine*, September 2003, 49.

3 Ibid.; emphasis in original.

4 Ibid.; emphasis in original.

5 Two good places to begin a study of John Muir's life and thought are Frederick Turner, *Rediscovering America: John Muir in His Time and Ours* (New York: Viking, 1985), and Linnie Marsh Wolfe, *Son of the Wilderness: The Life of John Muir* (New York: Knopf, 1951). Michael Cohen's *The Pathless Way: John Muir and American Wilderness* (Madison: University of

Wisconsin Press, 1984) is not so much a biography as it is an examination of Muir's spiritual and intellectual development as seen in the context of today's environmentalist debates. Likewise, Stephen Fox's *The American Conservation Movement: John Muir and His Legacy* (Madison: University of Wisconsin Press, 1985) explores Muir's life and thought within the context of the gradual emergence of America's interest in conservation.

6   John Muir, *The Story of My Boyhood and Youth* (Boston: Houghton Mifflin, 1913), 31.

7   Ibid., 1; emphasis added.

8   Cited in Turner, *Rediscovering America*, 30.

9   Muir, *Story of My Boyhood and Youth*, 63; emphasis added.

10   Ibid., 65, 75, and 113. Muir's biographical reflections include his memory that he "never tired listening to the wonderful whip-poor-will" (68), that he regarded his family's hog "a very wonderful beast" (75), and that "the next great flower wonder on which we lavished attention" was the cypripediums (121).

11   Ibid., 286.

12   John Muir, *My First Summer in the Sierra* (Boston: Houghton Mifflin, 1979), 125–27.

13   Cited in Cohen, *Pathless Way*, 18.

14   Ibid.

15   Cited in Turner, *Rediscovering America*, 187.

16   Cohen, *Pathless Way*, 259.

17   Cited in Fox, *American Conservation Movement*, 81. In November 1875, John Muir wrote that "when one comes out of the woods everything is novel. . . . Even our fellow beings are regarded with something of the same keenness and freshness of perception that is brought to a new species of wild animal." Cited in Cohen, *Pathless Way*, 225.

18   Ibid.

19   Cited in Cohen, *Pathless Way*, 212.

20   Ibid., 237.

21   Ralph Waldo Emerson, *The Complete Works of Ralph Waldo Emerson*, 12 vols. (New York: AMS Press, 1968), 1:62.

22   Ibid., 2:282.

23   Fox, *American Conservation Movement*, 6–7, 82. Thoughtful comparisons of Emerson's and Muir's thought can also be found in both Turner, *Rediscovering America*, and Cohen, *Pathless Way*.

24   John Muir, *The Mountains of California* (New York: Century, 1901), cited in Wolfe, *Son of the Wilderness*, 163; emphasis added.

25   Muir, *My First Summer in the Sierra*, 80.

26 Catherine Albanese, *Nature Religion in America* (Chicago: University of Chicago Press, 1990), 105. Albanese's discussion of Muir concludes with this paragraph:

> Hence, as a latter-day Transcendentalist, Muir championed, for the most part, the side of the Transcendentalist gospel that proclaimed the spiritual power in nature. His idealism—an apology to his once-and-former Calvinism—was a muted breed, more muted even than the idealism of Henry David Thoreau. Meanwhile, his embrace of nature went beyond Emerson and Thoreau in its sensuousness, in its sheer and unqualified delight in matter. Lord Sequoia and the sequoia sacrament had made of Muir a religious radical, seeing in the stuff of the earth the ultimacy that others had placed in the starry sky and in the God beyond the stars.

27 Muir, cited in Fox, *American Conservation Movement*, 82.

28 See the succinct overview of Muir's contributions to environmentalist thought in Bron Taylor and Jeffrey Kaplan, eds., *The Encyclopedia of Religion and Nature* (New York: Continuum, 2005). Both Cohen (*Pathless Way*) and Fox (*American Conservation Movement*) also provide extended overviews of Muir's relationship to the growth of environmental awareness in North America.

Chapter 4

1 Charles Darwin, *The Expression of the Emotions in Man and Animals* (London: HarperCollins, 1998), 284; emphasis added.

2 Steven Pinker, *How the Mind Works* (New York: W. W. Norton, 1997), 21.

3 Ibid., 358.

4 Ibid., 564. Pinker explicitly uses the words "wonder" and "awe" on pp. ix and 565 when contrasting purposeful and purposeless mental responses to the world.

5 Ibid., 525.

6 Ibid., 554.

7 Scott Atran, *In God We Trust: The Evolutionary Landscape of Religion* (New York: Oxford University Press, 2002), 57.

8 Richard Dawkins, *Unweaving the Rainbow: Science, Delusion, and the Appetite for Wonder* (New York: Houghton Mifflin, 1998), 264.

9 Ibid., 27.

10 Ibid., 114.

11 Konrad Lorenz, *On Aggression* (New York: Harcourt, Brace and World, 1963), 263.

12 The following summary of creative adaptation borrows freely from Don Browning's excellent discussion of this topic in *The Moral Context of Pastoral Care* (Philadelphia: Westminster Press, 1976), 75–90. Browning, seeking to develop a philosophical model that explains the role that counselors and therapists perform in culture, synthesizes a vast array of information about creative adaptation from evolutionary biology, cultural anthropology, and developmental psychology.

13 David Bakan, *The Duality of Human Existence* (New York: Rand McNally, 1966).

14 Ernest Schactel, *Metamorphosis: On the Development of Affect, Perception, Attention, and Memory* (New York: Basic Books, 1959).

15 Arthur J. Deikman, "Bimodal Consciousness," *Archives of General Psychiatry* 25 (December 1971): 481–89.

16 See Talcott Parsons's introduction to Max Weber, *The Sociology of Religion* (Boston: Beacon Press, 1963).

17 This summary of creative adaptation borrows heavily from Browning, *Moral Context of Pastoral Care*, 75–90.

18 Ibid., 18.

19 Bron Taylor, "John Muir," in Bron Taylor and Jeffrey Kaplan, eds., *The Encyclopedia of Religion and Nature* (New York: Continuum, 2005).

20 Clifford Geertz, *The Interpretation of Cultures* (New York: Basic Books, 1973), 90; emphasis added.

21 Peter Berger, *The Sacred Canopy: Elements of a Sociological Theory of Religion* (Garden City, N.Y.: Anchor Books, 1967), 25.

22 Ibid., 24–25, 33; emphasis in original.

23 Geertz, *Interpretation of Cultures*, 112.

24 Felicitas Goodman, *Ecstasy, Ritual, and Alternate Reality* (Bloomington: Indiana University Press, 1988).

25 Andrew Newberg, Eugene d'Aquili, and Vince Rause, *Why God Won't Go Away: Brain Science and the Biology of Belief* (New York: Ballantine Books, 2001), 34; emphasis added.

26 Ibid., 72.

27 Ibid., 89.

Chapter 5

1 Juan De Pascuale, "A Wonder Full Life," *Notre Dame Magazine*, September 2003, 49

2 Among the biographies of William James are Ralph Barton Perry, *The Life and Character of William James*, 2 vols. (Boston: Little, Brown, 1935); Gerald E. Myers, *William James: His Life and Thought* (New Haven,

Conn.: Yale University Press, 1986); Gay Wilson Allen, *William James* (New York: Viking, 1967); Howard Feinstein, *Becoming William James* (Ithaca, N.Y.: Cornell University Press, 1984); Cushing Stout, "The Pluralistic Identity of William James," *American Quarterly* 23 (May 1971): 135–52; and Linda Simon, *Genuine Reality: A Life of William James* (New York: Harcourt, Brace and Co., 1998).

3 Erik Erikson, *Young Man Luther* (New York: W. W. Norton, 1962), 67.

4 William James, in Henry James Jr., ed., *Letters of William James* (Boston: Kraus Reprint Co., 1969), 1:130.

5 William James, cited in Perry, *Life and Character of William James*, 1:136.

6 A discussion of Blood's nitrous oxide–induced mystical philosophy can be found in Hal Bridges, *American Mysticism* (New York: Harper and Row, 1970), 15–19.

7 James's initial publication on nitrous oxide appeared in *Mind* 7 (April 1882): 186–208. It also appears in an abridged form as "Subjective Effects of Nitrous Oxide," in *Altered States of Consciousness*, ed. Charles Tart (New York: Wiley, 1969), 367–70.

8 See Robert C. Fuller, *Stairways to Heaven* (Boulder, Colo.: Westview Press, 2000), 54–57, and *Religious Revolutionaries* (New York: Palgrave Macmillan, 2004), 138–49. See also Dmitri Tymoczko, "The Nitrous Oxide Philosopher," *Atlantic Monthly*, May 1996, 93–101. Although Tymoczko's article gives the mistaken impression that James frequently used nitrous oxide when there is no evidence to indicate that he ever used the gas more than his one initial experiment, the article does help to situate the experience within James's professional career and the larger cultural issues raised by the connection between drugs and mysticism.

9 William James, *Essays in Psychical Research* (Cambridge, Mass.: Harvard University Press, 1986), 131. The preface to this volume, written by Robert McDermott, is an excellent introduction to James's interest in psychical research. Readers might also wish to consult Gardner Murphy and Robert O. Ballou, eds., *William James on Psychical Research* (New York: Viking, 1960), and Eugene Taylor, *William James on Consciousness beyond the Margin* (Princeton, N.J.: Princeton University Press, 1996).

10 William James, cited in Myers, *William James*, 52.

11 William James, *The Varieties of Religious Experience* (Cambridge, Mass.: Harvard University Press, 1985), 307.

12 William James, *A Pluralistic Universe* (New York: E. P. Dutton, 1971), 264.

13 James, *Varieties of Religious Experience*, 15.

14 James, *Pluralistic Universe*, 266.

15 In an essay entitled "On a Certain Blindness in Human Beings," in *Essays on Faith and Morals*, ed. Ralph Barton Perry (New York: Meridian Books,

1962), James argued that our ethical failings stem from the tragic fact that our consciousness is so structured by immediate self-interest that we simply fail to recognize the needs and interests of those who are different from us. We best escape self-interest, James contends, when we suddenly and unexpectedly attain "a mystic sense of hidden meaning" or "the higher vision of an inner significance in what, until then, we had realized only in the dead external way" (268). James's formulation of what might be called an "ethics of appreciation" rather than an ethics of obedience to authority is thus highly reminiscent of Martha Nussbaum's contention that "wonder, as non-eudaimonistic as an emotion can be, helps move distant objects within the circle of a person's scheme of ends.... [Wonder responds] to the pull of the object, and one might say that in it the subject is maximally aware of the value of the object, and only minimally aware, if at all, of its relationship to her own plans." Nussbaum, *Upheavals of Thought: The Intelligence of the Emotions* (Cambridge, England: Cambridge University Press, 2001), 54.

16 James, *Pluralistic Universe*, 267.

17 Carol Zaleski, "Speaking of William James to the Cultured among His Despisers," in *The Struggle for Life: A Companion to William James's The Varieties of Religious Experience*, ed. Donald Capps and Janet Jacobs, (Princeton, N.J.: Society for the Scientific Study of Religion, 1996), 59. See also my discussion of James's role in American religious history in *Spiritual, but Not Religious* (New York: Oxford University Press, 2001), 129–35, and *Religious Revolutionaries* (New York: Palgrave Macmillan, 2004), 138–49.

Chapter 6

1 Aristotle, *Metaphysica* (New York: Random House, 1941), 689.

2 There are many fine introductions to the work of Jean Piaget. One of the most succinct is the summary provided in Henry Maier, *Three Theories of Child Development* (New York: Harper and Row, 1969). Readers might also wish to consult Richard Evans, *Jean Piaget: The Man and His Ideas* (New York: E. P. Dutton, 1973) or Mary Ann Spencer Pulaski, *Understanding Piaget* (New York: Harper and Row, 1971). Helpful assessments of Piaget's long-term impact on developmental psychology can be found in David Elkind and John Flavell, eds., *Studies in Cognitive Development: Essays in Honor of Jean Piaget* (New York: Oxford University Press, 1969).

3 In celebration of the centennial anniversary of Jean Piaget's birth, *Psychological Science* published a collection of articles assessing his legacy to the field of cognitive psychology. See *Psychological Science* 7 (July 1996): 191–

225. That same year Orlando Lourenço and Armando Machado published "In Defense of Piaget's Theory: A Reply to Ten Common Criticisms," *Psychological Review* 103 (January 1996): 143–64. Patricia Miller also provides a helpful overview of the current status of Piaget's contributions to the field in *Theories of Developmental Psychology*, 4th ed. (New York: W. H. Freeman, 2001).

4   William Charlesworth, "The Role of Surprise in Cognitive Development," in Elkind and Flavell, *Studies in Cognitive Development*, 257–314.

5   Ibid., 308.

6   See the excellent discussion of Piaget and "the world of possibilities" in Paul Harris, "On Not Falling Down to Earth: Children's Metaphysical Thinking," in *Imagining the Impossible: Magical, Scientific, and Religious Thinking in Children*, ed. Karl Rosengren, Carl Johnson, and Paul Harris (Cambridge, England: Cambridge University Press, 2000), 157–78.

7   Jean Piaget, *The Psychology of Intelligence* (London: Routledge and Kegan Paul, 1950), 148.

8   Jean Piaget and B. Inhelder, *The Growth of Logical Thinking from Childhood to Adolescence* (New York: Basic Books, 1958), 256.

9   See the excellent discussion of the development of metaphysical thought in Carl Johnson, "Putting Different Things Together: The Development of Metaphysical Thinking," in Rosengren, Johnson, and Harris, *Imagining the Impossible*, 179–211.

10   Robert Kegan, a self-professed follower of Piaget, warns that we must be careful to correct for the tendency of Piagetians to be principally concerned "about *cognition*, to the neglect of *emotion*; the *individual*, to the neglect of the *social*; the *epistemological*, to the neglect of the *ontological* (or concept, to the neglect of being); *stages of meaning-constitution*, to the neglect of *meaning-constitutive process*." See Robert Kegan, "There the Dance Is: Religious Dimensions of a Developmental Framework," in *Toward Moral and Religious Maturity*, ed. J. Fowler et al. (Morristown, N.J.: Silver Burdett, 1980), 406.

11   Jean Piaget, cited in Fernando Vidal, *Piaget before Piaget* (Cambridge, Mass.: Harvard University Press, 1994), 57.

12   Ibid.

13   Ibid., 192.

14   An excellent summary of the contributions that both self psychology and object relations theory have made to developmental psychology is Robert Galatzer-Levy and Bertram Cohler, *The Essential Other: A Developmental Psychology of the Self* (New York: Basic Books, 1993). See also the introductory section of Robert Coles, *The Spiritual Life of Children* (Boston: Houghton Mifflin, 1990).

15 Henry Guntrip, "Religion in Relation to Personal Integration," *British Journal of Medical Psychology* 42 (1969): 325.

16 See Heinz Kohut, *The Analysis of Self* (New York: International Universities Press, 1971).

17 D. W. Winnicott, *Playing and Reality* (London: Tavistock Publications, 1971), 14.

18 Ana-Marie Rizzuto, *The Birth of the Living God* (Chicago: University of Chicago Press, 1979), 193; emphasis added.

19 William James, "Reflex Action and Theism," in *The Will To Believe* (New York: Dover Publications, 1956), 127; emphasis in original.

20 Lawrence Kohlberg, "Continuities and Discontinuities in Childhood and Adult Moral Development Revisited," in *Life Span Developmental Psychology*, ed. R. Baltes and K. Schaie (New York: Academic Press, 1973), 202.

21 Ibid.

22 Martha Nussbaum, *Upheavals of Thought: The Intelligence of Emotions* (Cambridge, England: Cambridge University Press, 2001), 54.

23 Ibid., 55.

24 Robert Greenleaf, "Have You a Dream Deferred?," in *The Power of Servant Leadership*, ed. Larry Spears (San Francisco: Berret-Koehler, 1998), 108.

25 Carroll Izard, *Human Emotions* (New York: Plenum Press, 1977), 3.

26 Carroll Izard and Brian Ackerman, "Motivational, Organizational, and Regulatory Functions of Discrete Emotions," in *Handbook of Emotions*, 2nd ed., ed. Michael Lewis and Jeannette M. Haviland-Jones (New York: Guilford Press, 2000), 257.

27 Ibid.

28 Abraham Maslow, *Toward a Psychology of Being* (New York: D. Van Nostrand, 1968), 27

29 Ibid., 36.

30 Abraham Maslow, *Religions, Values, and Peak Experiences* (New York: Viking, 1970), 65; emphasis added.

31 Abraham Maslow, *The Farther Reaches of Human Nature* (New York: Viking, 1973), 264; emphasis added.

32 Ernest Schactel, *Metamorphosis: On the Development of Affect, Perception, Attention, and Memory* (New York: Basic Books, 1959), 177.

33 Ibid., 147.

34 Ibid., 240; emphasis added.

Chapter 7

1 Rachel Carson, *A Sense of Wonder* (New York: Harper and Row, 1956), 88.

2 The most thorough biography of Rachel Carson is Linda Lear, *Rachel*

Carson: Witness for Nature (New York: Henry Holt and Co., 1997). Paul Brooks also connects Carson's life and thought in his *The House of Life: Rachel Carson at Work* (Boston: Houghton Mifflin, 1972). Stephen Fox sets Carson's work into the larger sweep of modern environmental thought in his *The American Conservation Movement: John Muir and His Legacy* (Madison: University of Wisconsin Press, 1985), 292–99.

3 Cited in Fox, *American Conservation Movement*, 293.

4 Rachel Carson, cited in Lear, *Rachel Carson*, 338. It might be noted that Rachel Carson dedicated her most important book, *Silent Spring*, to Albert Schweitzer. Carson framed the letter of gratitude she received from Schweitzer and considered it her most cherished possession (see Lear, *Rachel Carson*, 438).

5 Rachel Carson, from *The Edge of the Sea* (Boston: Houghton Mifflin, 1955), 3.

6 Rachel Carson, *Silent Spring* (Boston: Houghton Mifflin, 1962), 249.

7 Rachel Carson, from the foreword to the original edition of *Under the Sea-Wind* (New York: Simon and Schuster, 1941).

8 Rachel Carson, from her National Book Award Acceptance Speech, cited in Brooks, *House of Life*, 127. The reversal of figure and ground characteristically produced by the emotion of wonder is exemplified in Carson's observation that "looking out over the cove I felt a strong sense of the interchangeability of land and sea in this marginal world of the shore, and of the links between the life of the two. There was also an awareness of the past and of the continuing flow of time, obliterating much that had gone before, as the sea had that morning washed away the tracks of the bird." See Brooks, *House of Life*, 170.

9 Rachel Carson, *The Sea around Us* (New York: Oxford University Press, 1951), cited in Fox, *American Conservation Movement*, 416.

10 Carson, *Edge of the Sea*, 7.

11 Lear, *Rachel Carson*, 284.

12 Rachel Carson, "Help Your Child to Wonder," *Woman's Home Companion*, July 1956, 46. See also Lear, *Rachel Carson*, 284.

13 Rachel Carson, address to Theta Sigma Phi sorority of women journalists in 1954, in Linda Lear, ed., *Lost Woods: The Discovered Writing of Rachel Carson* (Boston: Beacon Press, 1998), 163.

14 Rachel Carson, letter to Dorothy Freeman, cited in Lear, *Rachel Carson*, 311.

15 Carson, address to Theta Sigma Phi, 160.

16 When an elderly fundamentalist accused Rachel Carson of ignoring God and the Bible in her discussions of nature, she took the trouble to respond: "It is true that I accept the theory of evolution as the most logical

one that has ever been put forward to explain the development of living creatures on this earth. As far as I am concerned, however, there is absolutely no conflict between a belief in evolution and a belief in God as the creator. Believing as I do in evolution, I merely believe that is the method by which God created, and is still creating, life on earth. And it is a method so marvelously conceived that to study it in detail is to increase—and certainly never to diminish—*one's reverence and awe* both for the Creator and the process." See Brooks, *House of Life*, 9; emphasis added.

17 Carson, *Sense of Wonder*, 42–43.

18 Ibid., 88.

19 Carson, *Edge of the Sea*, 250.

Chapter 8

1 Martin Buber, cited in Nahum N. Glatzer, ed., *The Way of Response: Martin Buber* (New York: Schocken Books, 1966), 48.

2 Martin Buber, *Between Man and Man* (New York: Macmillan, 1948), 203–4; emphasis added.

3 Ibid., 204.

4 Martin Buber, cited in Glatzer, *Way of Response*, 47.

5 See Philip Wheelwright's assessment of Buber's philosophy, "Buber's Philosophical Anthropology," in *The Philosophy of Martin Buber*, ed. Paul Schlipp and Maurice Friedman (LaSalle, Ill.: Open Court, 1967), 69–96. In this essay Wheelwright comments,

> Since personhood essentially involves, both in existence and in its adequate conception, relationship to other persons, and since every genuine relationship is a relationship not with the crust of another's personality but with that other's power of responding and meeting, which is to say with the divinity that is the very core of that other person, it follows that the study of personhood necessarily involves a study or at least a questioning of that which transcends the personal, as the divine does the human. In short, philosophical anthropology implies, without prescriptive dogma, theology. The divinity of man cannot be understood as something existing all by itself, but only as the creature, or the reflection or emanation, of the divinity that is God. (85)

6 Martin Buber, *The Prophetic Faith* (New York: Macmillan, 1949) 46.

7 Martin Buber, *Moses* (Oxford, England: East West Library, 1946), 75.

8 Carl Rogers, *A Way of Being* (Boston: Houghton Mifflin, 1980), 16.

9 Carl Rogers, *On Becoming a Person* (Boston: Houghton Mifflin, 1961), 26.

10   Rogers, *Way of Being*, 8.

11   Ibid.

12   Ibid., 7.

13   Martin Buber, *I and Thou* (New York: Charles Scribner's Sons, 1970), 85.

14   Howard Gardner, *Intelligence Reframed* (New York: Basic Books, 1999), 60.

15   Ibid., 65.

16   For examples of recent humanities scholarship discussing the role of emotions in Asian cultures, see the articles in "Ethics and Emotions in South Asian Buddhism," a special issue of the *Journal of the American Academy of Religion* 71 (September 2003). See also Arjun Appadurai, "Topographies of the Self: Praise and Emotion in Hindu India," in *Language and the Politics of Emotion*, ed. Catherine Lutz and Lila Abud-Lughod (Cambridge, England: Cambridge University Press, 1990), 92–112; Harvey Aronson, *Love and Sympathy in Theravada Buddhism* (Delhi: Motilal Barasidass, 1980); Catherine Lutz, *Unnatural Emotions: Everyday Sentiments on a Micronesian Atoll and Their Challenge to Western Theory* (Chicago: University of Chicago Press, 1988); Krishna Sharma, *Bhakti and the Bhakti Movement: A Study in the History of Ideas* (New Delhi: Munshiram Manaharlal Publishers, 1987); June McDaniel, *The Madness of the Saints: Ecstatic Religion in Bengal* (Chicago: University of Chicago Press, 1989); Andrew Rawlinson, "Love and Meditation in the Bhakti Tradition," in *The Saints: Studies in a Devotional Tradition of India*, ed. Karine Schomer and W. H. McLeod (Berkeley: University of California Press, 1987), 53–58; and C. Gispert-Sauch, *Bliss in the Upanishads: An Analytical Study of the Origin and Growth of the Vedic Concept of Ananda* (New Delhi: Orientalia Publishers, 1977).

17   See Susan Schwartz, *Rasa* (New York: Columbia University Press, 2004), and Richard A. Shweder and Jonathan Haidt, "The Cultural Psychology of the Emotions: Ancient and New," in *Handbook of Emotions*, 2nd ed., ed. Michael Lewis and Jeannette M. Haviland-Jones (New York: Guilford Press, 2000), 397–416.

18   Robert Kegan, *The Evolving Self* (Cambridge, Mass.: Harvard University Press, 1982), 25.

19   The best overview of Keith Oatley's work on emotions is his highly regarded text coauthored with Jennifer Jenkins, *Understanding Emotions* (Malden, Mass.: Blackwell, 1996). His work on emotions and the arts can be found in Keith Oatley, "Creative Expression and Communication of Emotions in the Visual and Narrative Arts," in *Handbook of Affective Sciences*, ed. Richard J. Davidson, Klaus Scherer, and H. Hill Goldsmith (New York: Oxford University Press, 2003), 481–502.

20 See J. A. Russell, "A Circumplex Model of Affect," *Journal of Personality and Social Psychology* 39 (December 1980): 1161–78.

21 See S. Kaplan, "Environmental Preference in a Knowledge-Seeking, Knowledge-Using Organism," in *The Adapted Mind*, ed. J. Barkow, L. Cosmides, and J. Tooby (New York: Oxford University Press, 1993), 581–98.

22 Oatley, "Creative Expression," 490.

23 Leonard Meyer offers a helpful introduction to the philosophical subtleties underlying discussions of the aesthetic function of music in the first chapter of *Emotion and Meaning in Music* (Chicago: University of Chicago Press, 1956).

24 See the excellent literature review in Alf Gabrielsson and Patrick Juslin, "Emotional Expression in Music," in Davidson, Scherer, and Goldsmith, *Handbook of Affective Sciences*, 503–34.

25 Anthony Storr offers an excellent discussion of music from the standpoint of philosophical aesthetics in *Music and the Mind* (New York: Ballantine Books, 1992).

26 Robert Jourdain, *Music, the Brain, and Ecstasy* (New York: William Morrow, 1997), 330.

27 Ibid.

28 Ibid., 331.

29 Richard Lazarus and Bernice Lazarus, *Passion and Reason: Making Sense of Our Emotions* (New York: Oxford University Press, 1994), 129.

30 Ibid., 135.

31 G. H. Hardy, *A Mathematician's Apology* (Cambridge, England: Cambridge University Press, 1940), 24.

32 Henri Poincaré, cited in H. E. Huntley, *The Divine Proportion: A Study in Mathematical Beauty* (New York: Dover Publications, 1970), 1.

33 K. Weierstrass, cited in Huntley, *Divine Proportion*, 1.

34 John Keats, cited in Mario Livio, *The Golden Ratio: The Story of Phi, the World's Most Astonishing Number* (New York: Broadway Books, 2002), 231.

35 Huntley, *Divine Proportion*, 36; emphasis added.

36 Plato, *The Republic*, epigraph in Philip Davis and Reuben Hersh, *The Mathematical Experience* (Boston: Birkhauser, 1980).

37 Roger Penrose, *The Emperor's New Mind* (London: Vintage, 1990), 126.

38 Frans de Waal, epigraph in Robert Plutchik, *Emotions and Life: Perspectives from Psychology, Biology, and Evolution* (Washington, D.C.: American Psychological Association, 2003). It is interesting that Plutchik fails to list the emotion of wonder as a "primary" human emotion even though he acknowledges its central role in generating creative thought.

39 Ernst Mayr, *The Growth of Biological Thought* (Cambridge, Mass.: Harvard University Press, Belknap Press, 1982), 81.

40 Arthur Peacocke, "Sociobiology and Its Theological Implications," *Zygon* 19 (June 1984): 179. See also Arthur Peacocke, *Theology for a Scientific Age* (Minneapolis, Minn.: Fortress Press, 1993), especially the section "Asking 'Why?': The Search for Intelligibility and Meaning," 87–90.

41 Ursula Goodenough, *The Sacred Depths of Nature* (New York: Oxford University Press, 1998), 11.

42 Ibid., xvi; emphasis added.

43 Ibid., xvii.

44 John E. Smith, *Experience and God* (New York: Oxford University Press, 1998), 60; emphasis added.

45 Erich Fromm, *Psychoanalysis and Religion* (New Haven, Conn.: Yale University Press, 1950), 94; emphasis added.

46 For more information on the role of cognitive structures in shaping our experience (with an eye toward understanding the role that mediation and mystical practices play in altering this experience), see Jerome Bruner, *Beyond the Information Given* (New York: W. W. Norton, 1973).

47 There is no shortage of books that provide overviews of the basic types and goals of meditation. Among the better known are Claudio Naranjo and Robert Ornstein, *On the Psychology of Meditation* (New York: Viking, 1971), and Daniel Goleman, *The Varieties of the Meditative Experience* (New York: E. P. Dutton, 1977).

48 See Arthur J. Deikman, "Deautomatization and the Mystic Experience," *Psychiatry* 29 (November 1966): 324–38, reprinted in Charles Tart, ed., *Altered States of Consciousness* (New York: Wiley, 1969). Further exploration of the role of mediation and mystical practices in dismantling the generalized reality orientation can be found in Charles Tart, *States of Consciousness* (New York: E. P. Dutton, 1975), and Roland Fischer, "A Cartography of the Ecstatic and Meditative States," *Science*, November 26, 1971, 897–904.

49 Naranjo and Ornstein, *On the Psychology of Meditation*, 12.

50 Thich Nhat Hanh, *The Miracle of Mindfulness: A Manual on Meditation* (Boston: Beacon Press, 1976), 12; emphasis added. Hanh describes certain breathing exercises that can trigger awareness that "your breath is the wondrous method of taking hold of your consciousness" and explains that there are "wondrous questions" that intensify spiritual awareness (22, 69).

51 Herbert Benson, *The Relaxation Response* (New York: William Morrow, 1975); Herbert Benson and W. Proctor, *Beyond the Relaxation Response* (New York: Times Books, 1984).

52 Andrew Newberg, Eugene d'Aquili, and Vince Rause, *Why God Won't Go Away: Brain Science and the Biology of Belief* (New York: Ballantine Books, 2001).

53 See Richard Davidson and Julian Davidson, eds., *The Psychobiology of Consciousness* (New York: Plenum Press, 1980), and Daniel Goleman and Richard Davidson, *Consciousness, the Brain, States of Awareness, and Alternate Realities* (New York: Irvington, 1979).

54 Dean Hamer, *The God Gene: How Faith Is Hardwired into Our Genes* (New York: Doubleday, 2004).

55 William James, *The Varieties of Religious Experience* (Cambridge, Mass.: Harvard University Press, 1985), 302.

56 William James considered the experience of "cosmic consciousness" as studied by the Canadian psychiatrist Dr. R. M. Bucke to be an example of fully developed mystical awareness. It is important to note that Bucke described the prime characteristic of cosmic consciousness as "a consciousness of the cosmos, that is, of the life and order of the universe." Bucke seems to be suggesting that cosmic consciousness is characterized by the perception of an order of existence that somehow lies beyond or behind the world of everyday experience. Bucke goes on to acknowledge yet another trait shared by both mysticism and the emotion of wonder—that of engendering personal transformation. Bucke writes that "to this is added a state of moral exaltation, an indescribable feeling of elevation, elation, and joyousness, and a quickening of the moral sense, which is fully as striking and more important than is the enhanced intellectual power." Cited in James, *Varieties of Religious Experience*, 316.

57 Charles Tart, *On Being Stoned: A Psychological Study of Marijuana Intoxication* (Palo Alto, Calif.: Science and Behavior Books, 1971), 212.

58 Huston Smith, *Cleansing the Doors of Perception* (New York: Tarcher/Putnam, 2000), 22; emphasis added. In the same chapter Smith offers another prototypical mystical experience in which the person describes "a feeling of great peace and contentment seemed to flow through my entire body. . . . Words can't describe this. I feel an awe and wonder that such a feeling could have occurred to me" (28–29).

Chapter 9

1 Charles Honey, "Wonderful Christmas Wanderings," *Grand Rapids (Mich.) Press*, December 20, 2003, B1.

2 John E. Smith, *Experience and God* (New York: Oxford University Press, 1998), 60.

3   Joseph LeDoux, *The Emotional Brain* (New York: Simon and Schuster, 1996), 16.

4   Robert Solomon, *The Passions* (Garden City, N.Y.: Anchor Books, 1976), xviii.

5   Jean-Paul Sartre, cited in ibid., 232.

6   Solomon, *The Passions*, 239; emphasis added.

7   This was William James's point in his essay "The Sentiment of Rationality" when he argued that the natural sciences do not permit us to speak of reason as though it occurs somewhere outside the human brain. All cognition is affected by our emotions. It is simply a matter of which emotions and how hardwired or "plastic" the emotions happen to be. As James wrote in his famous essay "The Will to Believe," "if any one should thereupon assume that intellectual insight is what remains after wish and will and sentimental preference have taken wing, or that pure reason is what then settles our opinions, he would fly quite as directly in the teeth of the facts" (8). Both essays appear in *The Will to Believe* (New York: Dover Publications, 1956).

8   In *What Emotions Really Are: The Problem of Psychological Categories* (Chicago: University of Chicago Press, 1997), Paul Griffiths suggests that "higher cognitive emotions" involve much more cortical processing than basic emotions (which are largely governed by subcortical structures of the brain) and are more capable of being influenced by conscious thought. Although I am wary of all efforts to locate specific physiological centers of discrete emotions, Griffiths's distinction has merit and would certainly be applicable to wonder that is far more under the influence of conscious thought than the emotions typically listed as primary (e.g., fear, anger, disgust, distress).

9   George Lakoff and Mark Johnson, *Philosophy in the Flesh: The Embodied Mind and Its Challenge to Western Thought* (New York: Basic Books, 1999), 4.

10 Ibid., 102.

11 William LaFleur, "Body," in *Critical Terms for Religious Studies*. ed. Mark C. Taylor (Chicago: University of Chicago Press, 1998), 36.

12 Ibid.

13 Edward O. Wilson, *Sociobiology: The New Synthesis* (Cambridge, Mass.: Harvard University Press, Belknap Press, 1975), 55.

14 Lakoff and Johnson, *Philosophy in the Flesh*, 102–4. Lakoff and Johnson embrace what they call an "embodied realism" that examines humans' capacities to function successfully in their physical environments. They take it as a matter of descriptive fact that "evolution has provided us with adapted bodies and brains that allow us to accommodate to, and even

transform, our surroundings" (95). The brain's ability to accommodate to, and even transform, our surroundings is shaped by our embodiment in a particular culture that gives definition to our immediate self-consciousness. This functionalist understanding of human experience not only protects against reductionism but also provides a certain "evolutionary realism" for evaluative judgments: our capacity to function successfully in our world.

15 See Wilhelm Dilthey, *Introduction to the Human Sciences*, ed. Rudolf Makkreel and Frithjof Rodi (Princeton, N.J.: Princeton University Press, 1989). An explanation of Dilthey's contributions to the modern study of religion can be found in Guy Oakes, "Wilhelm Dilthey," in *Encyclopedia of Religion*, 2nd ed. (Detroit: Macmillan, 2005), 2352–53.

16 I have examined the role of fear and hate in the predisposition to apocalyptic thinking in *Naming the Antichrist: The History of an American Obsession* (New York: Oxford University Press, 1995), 8, 16, 28–29, 50–52, 92–94, 195.

17 Excellent discussions of the social and psychological forces affecting the communities that produced the apocalyptic thought contained in the biblical Book of Revelation can be found in Adela Yarbro Collins, *Crisis and Catharsis* (Philadelphia: Westminster Press, 1984) and *The Combat Myth in the Book of Revelation* (Missoula, Mont.: Scholars Press, 1976). Readers might also wish to explore the background of the Antichrist legend in Kenneth Grayston, *The Johannine Epistles* (Grand Rapids, Mich.: Wm. B. Eerdmans, 1984). The story of how social and psychological forces influenced the unique blend of conservative theology and apocalyptic suspicion underlying the Salem witchcraft trials is thoroughly explained in both Paul Boyer and Stephen Nissenbaum, *Salem Possessed: The Social Origins of Witchcraft* (Cambridge, Mass.: Harvard University Press, 1974), and Kai Erikson, *Wayward Puritans* (New York: Wiley, 1966).

18 Carroll Izard and Brian Ackerman, "Motivational, Organizational, and Regulatory Functions of Discrete Emotions," in *Handbook of Emotions*, 2nd ed., ed. Michael Lewis and Jeannette Haviland-Jones (New York: Guilford Press, 2000), 260.

19 Ibid.

20 William Clebsch, *American Religious Thought* (Chicago: University of Chicago Press, 1973), xvi.

21 In his classic essay "From Edwards to Emerson" (in *Errand into the Wilderness* [Cambridge, Mass.: Harvard University Press, Belknap Press, 1975], 185), Perry Miller reflected on the fact that "certain basic continuities persist in a culture . . . and underlie the succession of ideas." The continuities that so fascinated him concerned a strain of American spiri-

tuality that looked to "an indestructible element which was mystical, and a feeling for the universe which was almost pantheistic." Miller noted that Jonathan Edwards had been powerfully moved by his mystical-leaning "new sense" through which he claimed to discern the "images or shadows of divine things" in nature. Yet neither Miller nor William Clebsch (*American Religious Thought*) fully understood why Edwards resisted the "inherent mysticism, the ingrained pantheism" (Miller, "From Edwards to Emerson," 192) of these experiences and adhered instead to his inherited Puritan theological tradition.

22 William James, *The Varieties of Religious Experience* (Cambridge, Mass.: Harvard University Press, 1985), 51.

23 Ibid.

24 Ibid., 55, 59; emphasis in original.

25 Ibid., 66.

26 See the excellent discussion of this point in Paul Harris, "On Not Falling Down to Earth: Children's Metaphysical Thinking," in *Imagining the Impossible: Magical, Scientific, and Religious Thinking in Children*, ed. Karl Rosengren, Carl Johnson, and Paul Harris (Cambridge, England: Cambridge University Press, 2000).

27 This connection between "religious hypotheses" and significant human action is elaborated in William James's essay "Reflex Action and Theism," in *Will to Believe*, 131–32.

28 James, *Varieties of Religious Experience*, 23; emphasis in original.

29 William James, *A Pluralistic Universe* (New York: E. P. Dutton, 1971), 264.

30 Martin Buber, *The Prophetic Faith* (New York: Macmillan, 1949), 46.

31 Martin Buber, *Moses* (Oxford, England: East West Library, 1946), 75. See the discussion of this point in Maurice Friedman, *Martin Buber: The Life of Dialogue* (New York: Harper and Row, 1976), 116.

32 See the excellent discussion of this point in Carol Nemeroff and Paul Rozin, "The Makings of the Magical Mind: The Nature and Function of Sympathetic Magical Thinking," in Rosengren, Johnson, and Harris, *Imagining the Impossible*, 1–34. See also, in the same volume, Karl Rosengren and Anne Hickling, "Metamorphosis and Magic: The Development of Children's Thinking about Possible Events and Plausible Mechanisms," 75–98.

33 The personality theorist Gordon Allport argued that mature religious thought must have a heuristic quality. His point was that "fixed" religious ideas breed intolerance and even combativeness. Mature religiosity, he argued, views beliefs not as a closed system of truths but as hypotheses toward richer relationships with life. In his view, a heuristic faith has an open, eager, and fresh quality. See Gordon Allport, *The Individual and His*

Religion (New York: Macmillan, 1950). Readers might also wish to consider what role wonder plays in a person's transition from forms of religious thinking that James Fowler labels "conventional faith" to what he labels "universalizing faith." See James Fowler, *Stages of Faith: The Psychology of Human Development and the Quest for Meaning* (San Francisco: Harper and Row, 1981).

34 Rachel Carson, *The Edge of the Sea* (Boston: Houghton Mifflin, 1955), 250.
35 Marjorie Taylor and Stephanie Carlson, "The Influence of Religious Beliefs on Parental Attitudes about Children's Fantasy Behavior," in Rosengren, Johnson, and Harris, *Imagining the Impossible*, 247–68.
36 Juan De Pascuale, "A Wonder Full Life," in *Notre Dame Magazine*, September 2003, 49.

SUGGESTIONS FOR
FURTHER READING

There are many fine introductions to the study of emotion representing a wide range of academic disciplines. An excellent starting point is Robert Plutchik's *Emotions and Life: Perspectives from Psychology, Biology, and Evolution* (Washington, D.C.: American Psychological Association, 2003). Another helpful place to begin is Keith Oatley and Jennifer Jenkins, *Understanding Emotions* (Malden, Mass.: Blackwell, 1996).

Those who want to pursue the biological foundations of emotions should begin by consulting the relevant articles in Michael Lewis and Jeannette M. Haviland-Jones, eds., *Handbook of the Emotions*, 2nd ed. (New York: Guilford Press, 2000). Among the most important of these articles are Leda Cosmides and John Tooby, "Evolutionary Psychology and the Emotions"; Joseph LeDoux and Elizabeth Phelps, "Emotional Networks in the Brain"; and John Cacioppo, Gary Bernston, Jeff Larsen, Kirsten Poehlmann, and Tiffany Ito, "The Psychophysiology of Emotion." Further information on the evolutionary-adaptive functions of emotion can be found in Richard Lazarus, *Emotion and Adaptation* (New York: Oxford University Press, 1991), and Joseph LeDoux, *The Emotional Brain* (New York: Simon and Schuster, 1996). Additional descriptions of the neurophysiology of emotion can be found in Richard Lane and Lynn Nadel, eds., *Cognitive Neuroscience of Emotion* (New York: Oxford University Press, 2000).

Two foundational texts in the psychological study of emotion are Carroll Izard, *The Psychology of Emotions* (New York: Plenum Press,

1991), and Paul Ekman, *Emotion in the Human Face*, 2nd ed. (Cambridge, England: Cambridge University Press, 1982). Of further importance to understanding psychological approaches to emotion are Carroll Izard and Brian Ackerman, "Motivational, Organizational, and Regulatory Functions of Discrete Emotions," in Lewis and Haviland-Jones, *Handbook of Emotions*, and Sylvan Tomkins, "Affect as the Primary Motivational System," in *Feelings and Emotions*, ed. M. Arnold (New York: Academic Press, 1970).

An excellent introduction to the theoretical subtleties in the study of emotions is Aaron Ben-Ze'ev, *The Subtlety of Emotions* (Cambridge, Mass.: MIT Press, 2000). A critique of the biological approach to the study of emotion can be found in Rom Harré, ed., *The Social Construction of Emotions* (Oxford, England: Blackwell, 1986).

Several historical and cultural studies of emotion demonstrate the explanatory value of weak, moderate, or strong constructivist approaches to the study of emotion. A good beginning point is Peter N. Stearns and Carol Z. Stearns, "Emotionology: Clarifying the History of Emotions and Emotional Standards," *American Historical Review* 90 (October 1985): 813–36. A second point of introduction would be Richard A. Shweder and Jonathan Haidt, "The Cultural Psychology of the Emotions: Ancient and New," in Lewis and Haviland-Jones, *Handbook of Emotions*. Also recommended are John Corrigan, ed., *Religion and Emotion: Approaches and Interpretations* (New York: Oxford University Press, 2004), and John Corrigan, Eric Crump, and John Kloos, *Emotion and Religion: A Critical Assessment and Annotated Bibliography* (Westport, Conn.: Greenwood Press, 2000).

Among the most important philosophical treatments of the emotions are Martha Nussbaum, *Upheavals of Thought: The Intelligence of Emotions* (Cambridge, England: Cambridge University Press, 2001), and Robert Solomon, *The Passions* (Garden City, N.Y.: Anchor Books, 1976). A more far-reaching perspective on how knowledge concerning both physiological and neurophysiological processes alters our very understanding of philosophy can be found in George Lakoff and Mark Johnson, *Philosophy in the Flesh: The Embodied Mind and Its Challenge to Western Thought* (New York: Basic Books, 1999).

INDEX

Secondary emotions, 28–29

A Sense of Wonder (Carson), 108

Silent Spring (Carson), 102

Singer, Jerome, 19–20

Skinner, B. F., 19

Smith, Huston, 134, 177 (n. 58)

Smith, John E., 129, 134, 126

Socrates, 1, 129

Spiritual intelligence, 115–16

Spirituality: defined, 2; as encounter with the holy, 4; and feeling of absolute dependence, 3–4; rooted in wonder, 1–2. *See also* Religion

Stearns, Carol, 6

Stearns, Peter, 6

Surprise, 30, 84, 121–23, 124

Tart, Charles, 134

Taylor, Marjorie, 157

"Thou": and "I-Thou" relationship, 111–13, 155; world seen as, 92–93

Tomkins, Sylvan, 35–36, 37, 97

Tooby, John, 23, 26

The Varieties of Religious Experience (James), 76, 133, 149

Watson, John B., 19

Weber, Max, 62

Wilson, E. O., 143

Winnicott, D. W., 89, 90

Wonder: adaptive properties of, 12, 91, 95; in aesthetic experiences, 115–20; "appetite" for, 57–58, 63, 107, 154; classical Indian views of, 10–11, 29, 116–17; and Cognitive growth, 13, 86, 88, 91; cognitive limitations of, 92, 126, 151, 154–56; and contemplation of greater whole, 59, 60, 65–66, 81, 86–87, 92, 108–9, 116, 117, 126, 150; defined, 8, 33; difficulty classifying as an emotion, 32–33; distinguished from curiosity, 8, 86, 88, 125–26, 156; effect on empathy and compassion, 14, 93–96, 107; effect on perception and cognition, 32, 48–50, 53, 63–64, 91, 95, 96, 98, 99, 106, 117, 158; and fantasy, 91–92, 126, 151; fosters belief in nonvisible realities, 86–87, 91–92, 94, 151, 154–55; heuristic properties of, 96, 156–57; immediate luminousness of, 153–54; and interest, 12, 36–37; in interpersonal relationships, 111–15; and joy, 37, 97; in mathematics, 121–24; in meditation or mysticism, 129–32; mobilizing sustained interest, 36–37, 60, 97; and moral development, 14, 31–33, 94, 95; in music, 118–20; and mystery of existence, 43, 127–29; and nature, 46, 48–50, 75, 107–8; passive character of, 35, 38, 60; philosophical reasonableness of, 154–57; pragmatic evaluation of, 153–58; prototypical characteristics of, 30–31, 33–34, 54, 81; receptivity and, 62–63; ritualization of, 66, 68; in scientific inquiry, 124–28; scientific neglect of, 11, 31, 54, 59, 86–87

Zaleski, Carol, 79